WITHOUT
POWER OR GLORY

*Dedicated to Saoirse, and the life
she has ahead of her.*

WITHOUT POWER OR GLORY

The Green Party in Government in Ireland (2007-2011)

Dan Boyle

NEW ISLAND

WITHOUT POWER OR GLORY
First published 2012
by New Island
2 Brookside
Dundrum Road
Dublin 14

www.newisland.ie

Copyright © Dan Boyle, 2012

The author has asserted his moral rights.

PRINT ISBN: 978-1-84840-131-0
EPUB ISBN: 978-1-84840-177-8
MOBI ISBN: 978-1-84840-178-5

British Library Cataloguing Data. A CIP catalogue record for this book is
available from the British Library

Typeset by JM InfoTech INDIA
Cover design by Nina Lyons
Printed by Bell & Bain Ltd., Glasgow

New Island received financial assistance from
The Arts Council (An Comhairle Ealaíon), Dublin, Ireland

10 9 8 7 6 5 4 3 2 1

Contents

Acknowledgements

I would like to thank New Island Books for the faith that they placed in this book. I'm hugely appreciative of the patient editing done by Eoin Purcell and Dr Justin Corfield. Special gratitude is due to Kevin Rafter who encouraged me to have this book published. I'm also grateful to Katrina Doherty who read an early draft, and to Niamh FitzGibbon who kindly gave me the space that allowed me to write the initial chapters. The comprehensive notes of Niamh Allen, former Parliamentary Group Secretary to the Green Party, have been an invaluable resource.

My final thanks go to those with whom I've shared these experiences. I hope that this book may help to create a better understanding of why we did what we did, trying to do the right things for the right reasons.

Introduction

Brian Lenihan beckoned me from the Seanad chamber into the adjoining ante-room. He then proceeded to berate me in front of about a dozen Department of Finance officials. His fury was immense, lapsing into incoherence as he followed questions with further questions, the answers to which he suspected he already knew. 'What do you think you are playing at?' 'You must think you are very clever?' I took the barrage passively initially, reminding myself that this wasn't a very well man, and a man who was under considerable pressure.

However, the relentlessness made me respond in kind. As we shouted at each other, he worked his way to what he felt was his *coup de grâce*: 'That is why your party is responsible for everything that is wrong with this country.' I stared at him in disbelief, said no more, and went back into the Seanad chamber.

The arrogance and denial in that statement had stunned me into silence. It encapsulated how Fianna Fáil thought of the Green Party. Even now, when we were no longer a part of government, we were expected to do Fianna Fáil's bidding. To them, we were the bit players who were not expected to change the script.

The Seanad was having its final sitting before the general election in February 2011. The Dáil had risen, with the sole remaining business being the passage of the Finance Bill: the most savage Finance Bill in the history of the State.

Constitutional niceties demanded that the Dáil be open to being recalled should the Seanad propose any changes to the bill. The political reality, though, was that the now minority Fianna Fáil government, acting through the Minister for Finance, was not going to allow any changes to be made.

Intransigence of this nature was always part of Irish political machismo. In the case of the Seanad dealing with a Finance Bill, it was also somewhat unnecessary. The Seanad does not have the power to amend the legislation in the case of a bill of a financial nature, but can only recommend changes. Making any such recommendation would have meant recalling the Dáil.

As leader of the Green group in the Seanad, I didn't necessarily think that recalling the Dáil was such a bad thing. It was an important time in the political and economic history of the country. The Finance Bill was an important part of that process. To come back again might have improved the bill before the country embarked on a general election that would be badly informed on so many factors anyway.

The Labour Party suggested a change in the bill. The change would require that bonus payments given to executives of the all but nationalised financial institutions would be published. It was something that we felt we could support. Much of the public anger that was persisting in relation to banking centred around issues of continuing lack of responsibility and the perception that those who had caused the problem were still enriching themselves.

The motion wasn't that well written in our opinion, but we were prepared to co-operate on rewriting it and having it re-submitted for the report stage of the bill. When the order paper was produced, it caused a great deal of panic within Fianna Fáil. The vote would be close. This was the reason for Brian Lenihan's outburst.

The constitutional confines in which the Seanad operates means that no recommendations can be made that impact on the cost assumptions behind a Finance Bill. This means that decisions on taxation, revenue raising, or where the axe may have to fall are excluded from consideration by senators. This small point about banking might not have been the issue on which to make a stand, even though it remained a point worth making.

In the end, the motion was defeated by 26 votes to 25. The 24 Fianna Fáil senators were joined by Fiona O'Malley and Eoghan Harris, and thus the Dáil was spared the indignity of having to examine the Finance Bill one more time.

***

Much like our relationship with the wider electorate, our action in the Seanad, even with a real motive, only seemed to alienate everyone. Fianna Fáil, who already hated our decision to leave government, now hated us even more, as did the other parties, despite being given their long-demanded election.

Being able to please no one had plagued us since we had made our decision to leave government in November. 'Why not leave immediately?' we were asked. 'Why stay in Cabinet when you've called time on being in government?' 'Why indicate a preference for an election from January when you didn't possess the means for bringing that about?' 'Why support a package of measures during this time which, by their very nature, would be subject to widespread public disapproval?'

The following chapters attempt to answer these questions and more. Some questions can't be answered satisfactorily, because some things we simply got wrong. Being in government at the time of the biggest economic challenges in the history of the State was an experience that chastened us all, but provided valuable lessons that can help point to a more sustainable future.

This final meeting of the Seanad took place on January 29th. The maelstrom that had been life in government and Irish politics reminded me of newspaper article I had written in the aftermath of the general election in 2007. The intense personal experiences that I underwent then caused me to remember a line from the Talking Heads song, 'Once In A Lifetime':

And you may ask yourself, well, how did I get here?

How we, both as a party and as a country, 'got here' is the question that seeks resolution in these chapters.

1 | Ready For Government?

We went into this with our eyes open. Our break-through of winning six seats in the 2002 election saw our attention move for the first time to the idea of being in government. Local government elections in 2004 were also relatively successful, after which preparations began in earnest.

Throughout the party there was widespread expectation that being in government should be part of our continuing journey. There was also general agreement regarding the policy and the strategic approach that we would take. Personal expectations would be put aside and dealt with when they had to be.

Within the 22nd Dáil, we were seen to have performed well, operating with an eagerness and an enthusiasm that showed up the tired politics being offered by the more traditional political parties. The policy agenda seemed to be very much on our wavelength, and climate change became a regular topic of interest to a media that hungrily sought new angles through which to present Irish politics. Our opinion poll ratings crept ever upwards, peaking at 8%.

And yet those of us who had been through previous election campaigns knew that our opinion poll ratings had to be high if we were to withstand the spillage in support that always occurred during a general election. Part of this spillage came from a basic lack of political organisation. The

Greens remained an amateur political grouping. Our position on refusing corporate donations meant that we never had the resources to compete with larger political parties. Our small membership meant that we could never meet the challenge of the last week of intensive canvassing that worked so much against us.

To try and avoid this repeating pattern from previous election campaigns, the party established two internal committees: an electoral committee, which was an electoral task force chaired by John Gormley as Party Chair, and a policy committee, which was known initially as 'the Bütikofer Committee'. The second committee was called after a contribution made by Reinhard Bütikofer, then chair of the German Greens, who spoke at our 2004 Members' Convention in Galway about how the German Greens had prepared to become a party of government. In 2005, this process was further added to when the Finnish Green Minister for the Environment, Pekka Haavisto, spoke at the Party Convention in Cork.

In leading the electoral task force, John Gormley was helping to define the role of the Party Chairperson. Irish Greens, like most of our international counterparts, had been wary of formal leadership structures, but the failure to have someone on whom the media could focus was something that had to be changed. In 2001, Trevor Sargent was elected as the first party leader with Mary White as his deputy. In 2002, the new leadership was complete when John Gormley was elected as the first Party Chairperson.

The electoral task force went about the business of seeing candidates selected in every constituency. Each constituency was then prioritised as regards whether a Dáil seat was a possibility, whether a city/county council seat was possible in the short term, whether a town council seat could be brought about, or whether it was just a matter of giving voters in a constituency the opportunity of voting Green with no expectation of any electoral payback. The meagre resources of the Party were allocated according to these criteria, although the task force took it upon itself to standardise election materials such as posters and leaflets, again something that had been left to local candidates' discretion in previous elections.

The Bütikofer Committee met confidentially. Its remit was to examine the policy scope of the party, to fill in those areas where policies were not in existence or not deemed to be substantial enough. For the most part, the committee was charged with making the Green Party's policies more voter-friendly. Membership of this committee was tight. Eamon Ryan and I were members, as was the party's General Secretary Dermot Hamilton, the Head of Research Carol Fox, the Parliamentary Group Secretary Colm O'Caomhanaigh and Lucille Ryan O'Shea for the party's national executive.

In parallel to this, from 2005 on, the party had published a number of policy-position papers on subjects such as community development, care of the elderly and pensions, child care and pre-school education, transport and equality and civil rights issues. The appointment by the Houses of the Oireachtas of a parliamentary researcher to each TD proved to be a great help.

The results of this help could be seen in practical policy as well as theoretical policy development. By way of example, Sue Duke and Claire Byrne, working in Eamon Ryan's office, helped to pioneer a schools competition: 'No Logo', which loosely referenced the book by Naomi Klein, and set about encouraging a better understanding of how goods are produced and how local production is invariably better.

The competition had a considerable take up, which further helped in boosting the party's profile.

Back in our parliamentary offices, we found the thorniest of policy areas was that of economics. The hottest potato was that of the corporate tax rate. In the 1997 election we had argued for a 17.5% rate. In 2002, our argument was for a 15% rate, but in the meantime the questioning of the corporate tax rate had come to be seen as heresy, particularly within the media. As economics spokesperson, I argued that to hang ourselves on this issue would be to distract attention from the other more radical things we were saying in relation to economics. My view did prevail, but not before some heated debate at our party conference.

John Gormley was especially nervous about how our economic policy would be perceived. Representing the mostly leafy suburbs of Dublin South East, John realised that we shouldn't go out of our way to unnecessarily antagonise middle-class voters. His apprehension was added to by sharing a constituency with the by then leader of the Progressive Democrats Michael McDowell, who wasted few opportunities to taunt the Greens with his charges of our being economically illiterate.

Before the 2002 General Election, as the party's economic spokesperson, I reacted to a *Financial Times* story that claimed that Ireland was now the most globalised economy in the world. In a press release I said that this should be no source of pride:

> *What this report indicates is how dangerously open Ireland's economy has become, how it is most likely to be affected by declining international circumstances, and how we rely to too great an extent on foreign directed investment.*

*Two lessons should attach to this report, but nei-
ther lesson is likely to be given any consideration by
our economically callous government. The first lesson to
note is the continuing failure to produce a sustainable,
indigenous economy. The second lesson is the failure to
realise that short-term economic prosperity, brought
about through slavish adherence to globalisation, is
often bought at the expense of the world's developing
countries.*

This press release would be referred to on a number of
occasions by Fianna Fáil and Fine Gael during the 2002 and
2007 elections as evidence of the Greens being flaky on the
economy. I don't regret making the statement, as the very
openness of the Irish economy has been one of the factors
that subsequently brought us to our current economic situation.

The other touchy issue was that of Europe. We had
consistently advocated 'No' votes in the various referenda
on the European Union accession treaties, arguing that
the democratic deficit within the EU had to be addressed
before attempts to deepen the EU should be made. The
defeat of the Treaty of Nice in 2001 had panicked the political establishment in Ireland, and indeed throughout Europe.
The Irish Greens, despite this, were also a minority within
European Green thinking as to how the EU should develop.
While views similar to the Irish were held by the Swedes
and British, most European thinking was being led by the
Germans and the French.

That said, Irish Greens tried to be proactive in our
opposition to European treaty referenda. Prior to the first
Nice referendum, John Gormley had been an active participant in the Constitutional Convention chaired by former

French President Giscard d'Estaing. After the defeat of Nice I, the Green Party fully participated in the newly established National Forum on Europe, which involved many public meetings throughout the country. Despite this, there was also an understanding that, if in government, our position on Europe would not hold.

John Gormley was also particularly exercised with another issue. Should an opportunity to be in government arise, whom would the Green Party representatives in the Cabinet be? There would be an expectation of having two Cabinet Ministers and two Ministers of State, which was the representation achieved by similar sized political parties in previous governments.

As a parliamentary group, we had yet to confront the difficulties that would come from a clash of personal ambitions. We tended to get on well with each other. The closest thing to distrust that existed was between Paul Gogarty and Eamon Ryan, where Paul was unhappy with the way that Eamon had handled a failed bid to be a candidate for the presidency in 2004.

The classic ideological split that has existed in green parties, between the fundamentalists ('fundis') and the realists ('realos'), didn't really exist any more in the Irish Green Party. There were of course traditionalists, but there seemed to be a unity of purpose: the party was in the business of seeking power to bring about change.

***

Much of the election preparation centred on what seemed to be an unending series of meetings involving NGOs and interest groups – interest groups that previously had sought to have as little to do with the Green Party as possible. A good example of this would be the regular meetings that were held with the Irish Banking Federation. A particular meeting in 2006 was attended by Eamon Ryan and me. We brought up the question of the efficacy and economic sanity of issuing 110% mortgages, and the general lack of sustainability that seemed to exist in property market; a market the banks seemed intent on inflating further. The response to our concerns was both arrogant and condescending. We didn't understand banking, we were told, besides which the market would correct itself in a relatively painless manner.

Around the same time, with party leader Trevor Sargent, we were summoned to meet with Brian Goggin, Chief Executive of the Bank of Ireland, and two of his senior colleagues. The meeting took place in his suite of offices at the bank's headquarters on Baggot Street. We absorbed the opulence of the décor and the furniture, although we also enjoyed the fine food and wine that was supplied. It was clear that we were in the midst of one of the power centres of Irish life.

Our time was tight with a vote in the Dáil looming, but the time was used to probe us on whether we were 'sound' on banking issues. We were being royally wined and dined; an extremely sumptuous affair, although I suspect it was just another meal for the Bank of Ireland executives. At the end, it seemed we had met with their approval, until we had returned to Leinster House, when Trevor Sargent received an irate phone call from Brian Goggin berating him for not clearly stating our policy to introduce a 5% bank levy in the meeting. Our experience of the arrogance of banks and bankers was even then becoming far too prevalent.

Even with environmental NGOs, our relationships were far less robust than they should have been. Other political parties co-exist well with NGOs and interest groups, a classic case being the relationship between the Labour Party and the trade unions. Environmental NGOs, especially those in which Green Party members held senior positions, seemed anxious to be as apolitical as possible, perhaps over-compensating when it came to the Green Party.

The Bütikofer Committee experienced a name change in 2006, subsequently being referred to within the party as 'the Hamilton Committee'. The party's General Secretary, Dermot Hamilton, had died from a heart attack in January 2006, and the name change was to honour his memory within the party.

Dermot Hamilton was the Green Party's second General Secretary. Like his predecessor, Stiofán Nutty, he had been part of Trevor Sargent's constituency organisation in Dublin North. This group, having successfully elected Trevor in every general election since 1992, had long proved itself to be the best politically organised and managed Green group in the country. Stiofán, and later Dermot, sought to bring these qualities to the national party organisation.

Earlier in his political life, Dermot had been a member of Fianna Fáil, where the principles of ground-level politics had been ingrained into him; principles he sought to transfer to the Greens. His death, at the incredibly young age of 48, was a huge shock to the party and its members.

His replacement was Donal Geoghegan. Donal had applied for the General Secretary position twice before with my encouragement. I was slow to encourage him again lest he was once more unsuccessful, but ultimately he was. His appointment was something of a departure for the party as he hadn't been a party member. He brought with him experience of the Community and Voluntary sectors, and with that an intimate involvement in the social partnership process.

Donal's appointment as Party General Secretary also saw him take responsibility for the Hamilton committee. He did this well, ensuring that its deliberations never became known in the most open of political parties. This sensitivity was required because the subtext of the work of the committee was to prioritise the policies of the party, and consider how those policies might be addressed in the context of any negotiations occurring should the party participate in government.

The 25th anniversary of the founding of the party took place on December 3rd, 2006. An event was organised for the Central Hotel, Exchequer Street in Dublin. It was to be the launch of a book, *A Journey to Change*, marking the history of the party to date. It was at that hotel on that date in 1981 that an exploratory public meeting was held, which led to the establishment of a Green Party in Ireland.

In May 2006, I had discussed at various levels within the party the need to mark this date. The book was thought to be a good way of achieving that goal. My role, admittedly largely self-appointed, was to act as an overseeing editor on the publication, sourcing 25 representative members to write personal observations on their involvement in the party. Under our so politically correct approach to these things, I had to ensure that there was an appropriate balance between older and newer members, male and female, elected and volunteer, while including contributors from a range of geographical locations. I then wrote chronologically linked, themed chapters between each contribution, sketching how the party had evolved during the period.

Because time was short it required several people to put the publication together. I was greatly helped by my parliamentary researcher Laura Wipfler. She worked with my friend, and party stalwart from Cork, Sean O'Flynn, as sub-editor, while my secretary Edel Boyce helped with typing the manuscript. This was harder than it needed to be, because in order to short-circuit the process even further I had taken my Dictaphone on holiday with me in order to dictate several of the chapters. Others with me got more benefit from the Black Sea sun.

In any case, after this truncated process, the launch of the book was a significant event. Noted broadcaster John Bowman had kindly agreed to do the launch. Again we fretted about how to thank him for making himself available. We gave him a voucher for a well-known restaurant, but worried even then that the value of the voucher might have been seen as an attempt to curry favour.

The evening was very much a Green Party occasion. Founder members Christopher Fettes and Máire Mullarney were in attendance. Patricia McKenna's children played in front of the microphones in a way that seemed to bother no one, although I did make a caustic quip that they seemed to have learned from their mother how to disrupt events.

Trevor Sargent as party leader spoke, and was followed by John Bowman who, as a political historian, spoke well on the context of the Greens in Irish politics. As author-cum-editor, I finished proceedings and then we all headed off, pleased with what we had accomplished.

There wasn't much of a media presence at the launch. Harry McGee, then of the *Irish Examiner*, had been commissioned to write an independent overview of the book, and very fair it read. Others of a more political bent attended that evening. I had extended invitations to Oireachtas colleagues, and several came along. Pat Rabbitte, leader of the Labour Party, was there, partly out of an interest in books on political history, but largely I suspect because he wanted to encourage the Greens to become a firm part of a rainbow coalition after the impending election.

The Dublin South West constituency was well represented that evening. My friend Charlie O'Connor, Fianna Fáil TD for there (or Tallaght, as he constantly referred to it in his Dáil speeches) came along. Charlie and I had worked together several years previously with the National Youth Federation, and now found ourselves in Dáil Éireann together. Also present was Charlie's greatest political rival, his Fianna Fáil stablemate Conor Lenihan. I have no doubt that Conor also had an interest in the publication, but he also saw himself as a mover, and he wanted to be a person who could keep a door open for the Greens with Fianna Fáil should the need arise.

First time Fine Gael TD Fergus O'Dowd was there. We had struck up a good relationship, and I'm certain that he wasn't motivated by any need to be on a scouting mission for his party. To top things off, Senator Joe O'Toole came along, as did two independent TDs. Tony Gregory, who was whip of the independents within the Technical grouping in the Dáil, and with whom I had struck up a strong working relationship, was there. With him was Finian McGrath, independent TD for Dublin North Central. He was also someone with whom we got on well, but in Finian's case affinity was something of value to himself, as the then substantial Green vote in that constituency would determine who would win a final seat in what was to become a three seater. To be fair to him, it was a strategy that was to prove successful as he was to see off Labour, Sinn Féin and the Greens.

Most people who were present on that evening had their minds turned to an impending general election. It had been four and half years since the previous general election, and a new election was likely to be called at any time. The

Fianna Fáil/Progressive Democrat government was sitting uneasily, while the accession of Michael McDowell into the leadership of the Progressive Democrats exacerbated this situation. Bertie Ahern's evidence to the Mahon Tribunal, as Taoiseach, stretched credibility to the limit. A few days after our book launch, the Minister for Finance introduced what was to be the final budget of that administration. It was a giveaway budget – an election budget – with public expenditure dangerously increased by over 14%. After the Christmas recess, it would become a question of when the election would be called.

The Green party attempted to read the political climate. As ever with Irish politics, it was difficult to interpret. Even in advance of the election, efforts were ongoing to change the party from one of protest and opposition to a party of government. What the party was doing and how it was doing it was shifting perceptibly.

The fact that the party now had six TDs gave us access to large-scale State funding for the first time; something we used to the maximum degree. Regular newsletters were distributed in all six constituencies. Merchandising, in the form of umbrellas, mugs and campaign buttons, became more prevalent. Among the products being offered was a reusable jute bag. It was emblazoned with the party logo, and the legend: 'Ready for Government'. It was without a question mark.

2 | The 'Change' Election

Despite a succession of events that seemed to point to an election earlier in 2007, Bertie Ahern as Taoiseach was intent on repeating what had become a well-established pattern for him: remaining in office for as long as possible. In the first instance, this delay enabled all political parties to organise their party conferences in Spring 2007, each used as an election springboard.

The Greens' conference took place at the end of February at the Galway Bay Hotel. Increasing levels of professionalism were apparent in how Green Party conferences were being organised, with considerable resources being applied to make the event as visual as possible. The set was specially manufactured. Key individuals such as Karen Devine from Louth and former Party General Secretary Stiofán Nutty, as well as the party's indispensible administrator Alison Martin, worked full time at ensuring the event was as good as it could be.

The morale amongst party members in Galway was excellent. The talk was of government. There was an expectant air. Trevor's leader's speech caught this feeling well. In the oratorical stakes, however, he found himself being outshone by John Gormley's contribution as Party Chair, in his soon-to-become-infamous 'Planet Bertie' speech.

The speech was very well written, extremely well delivered and very, very funny. What we didn't know at the time was that it left many hostages to fortune. At the time, though, it was received rapturously by the party members, and proved to be an ideal tonic for those about to be knocking on doors. In it, he said:

> On Planet Bertie you can sign blank cheques, because everyone does it apparently. On Planet Bertie you can spend the average industrial wage on make-up. On Planet Bertie you can save €50,000 without a bank account. And on Planet Bertie climate change doesn't exist…
>
> It is so strange and so alien to our sensibilities that it's a planet that we Greens would like to avoid. For let there be no doubt, we want Fianna Fáil and the PDs out of government.

He got much pleasure in describing Michael McDowell, (whose tongue lashings he frequently had to suffer), as the 'Tammy Wynette of Irish politics – standing desperately behind his man Bertie'. Perhaps the most telling phrase in the speech wasn't about political invective at all, but a stark, honest admission that 'I cannot bear the thought of another five years in opposition.'

John may have been thinking out loud, but he wasn't saying anything that the rest of us in the parliamentary party weren't thinking. John, along with Trevor, Ciarán Cuffe, the former MEP Nuala Ahern and I, were all first elected to public office in the local council elections of 1991. With the exception of Paul Gogarty, we were all in our mid-to-late forties. Collectively, we wanted the opportunity of being in government to make the changes for which we had long campaigned.

The anti Fianna Fáil/Progressive Democrat feeling was predominant at the party conference. However, that antipathy wasn't to the point of exclusion. Not many in the party would definitely rule out talking to Fianna Fáil if that should become necessary.

In March, the party received a fillip when Brian Wilson was elected as the first Green member of the Northern Ireland Assembly. Brian was one of three councillors elected on the same day. All (Brian, Ciaran Mussen and Bill Corry) had a previous profile as independents, and all had also been members of other political parties, ranging from Alliance to the Workers Party. They were the first people to be elected under a Green banner in Northern Ireland. As an all-island party, Green members took great heart from these results.

As the month of April was closing, there still seemed to be no sign that the Dáil would be dissolved. The President was due to make a foreign visit and would be unavailable for a number of days, possibly requiring the Presidential Commission to be called into being.

Then, early on the morning of Sunday, April 29th, Ahern called the President at Arás an Úachtarán, and sought a dissolution of the Dáil. This approach was something of a departure, as the Taoiseach had decided to ask the President on a non-sitting day of the Dáil, so not informing the House of his decision. No one seemed to mind, though. Everyone was ready for the off.

We felt that we were sufficiently prepared. It would be the first general election where there would be a Green Party candidate in every Dáil constituency: 43 in total, as Trevor Sargent, as party leader, agreed to have a running mate – the popular local councillor Joe Corr. There wasn't an expectation that a second seat could be won here, but a good vote might make that possible in a future election.

It was a strong team. Six outgoing TDs, 11 city or county councillors, 3 town councillors and a former MEP. Over a quarter of our candidates were women, which wasn't bad, but could have been better. The goal was not only to retain the existing number of Green TDs, but also to extend the number of Greens in the Dáil to at least ten. Justifiable potential gains were seen in Carlow/Kilkenny, Wicklow, in Louth and in Galway West.

Our policy platform aside from our environmental concerns were centred around political reform, and being the party that was different – the party that didn't have the baggage of the others. While we articulated a different economic vision, we were aware that economic issues would play little part in this campaign.

The mood music at the start of the campaign was that the outgoing government was not going to be re-elected. However, one commentator alone, Shane Coleman, then working with the *Sunday Tribune*, had written that it could be possible with the addition of the Green Party. That possibility was as far as it could be from our collective mind.

The general perception was that, with Fianna Fáil having been in Government since 1997, a change was needed. Storm clouds from the Mahon Tribunal were hanging over the Taoiseach. Michael McDowell's new leadership of the Progressive Democrats was seen as being less than assured, with the media portraying him in 'Grand Old Duke of York' terms: leading his men up the hill and then promptly marching them back down again.

The opposition, in particular Fine Gael, had expectations of gains, having sunk to one of their lowest levels of support and Dáil numbers in the election of 2002. Labour, not without difficulty within its own ranks, had decided to fully hitch itself to the Fine Gael wagon. This had been formalised in the Mullingar Accord, in effect a joint election platform. All political parties besides the Green Party had said that they would not participate in government with Sinn Féin. These positions left the Greens free to pursue an independent line with regard to participation in the next government. It was a line that required considerable nuance.

While the government parties were expected to lose support, it wasn't expected that there would be a collapse in their support. Despite a growing distrust of politics, especially as it was being practised by Fianna Fáil, there was still a goodwill feeling with the economy, which on the surface seemed to be continuing to prosper.

This pervasive feeling of economic well-being for many led to the 2007 general election being almost free of issues. The first week of the campaign was dominated by the character of Bertie Ahern as Taoiseach. Before the election announcement was made, evidence from the Mahon Tribunal had been leaked that showed him in the poorest of lights. With the holding of the election, hearings of the tribunal were suspended. With no opportunity to analyse this information, the allegations became the focus of much political mud-slinging during the election campaign itself.

When the allegations first arose the Progressive Democrats were faced with a decision as to whether they should remain in government or not. That they chose to remain seemed to be impacting on them very badly in the election campaign.

Early opinion polls in the campaign showed Fine Gael and Labour gaining at the expense of Fianna Fáil. Despite the anti-Bertie, anti-Fianna Fáil mood, Greens were either static or slipping slightly in the polls. An element of panic was starting to emerge within the senior ranks of the party. Several days into the campaign, a meeting was organised, largely by teleconference, of the Green parliamentary party and our electoral team. While we were anticipating a squeeze, to have it happen so early in the campaign was worrying. Not to be gaining from anti-Fianna Fáil sentiment was bad in itself, but a Fine Gael surge would not only threaten hoped-for additional seats, but also threaten our ability to maintain our current parliamentary size. We knew that our advance in 2002 had largely been at the expense of Fine Gael, due to the perceived weakness of that party. In fact, all four Green seat gains in 2002 had been made at Fine Gael's expense. Any Fine Gael recovery would threaten our ability to advance. As we were all canvassing, the meeting was somewhat surreal and slightly farcical. Voices and contributions were coming in and out. There was no doubt that we needed to refocus the direction of the campaign and find a way to change tack. What was less clear was what change should be made, and how that was to be accomplished.

As a result of the meeting, and mainly at Trevor Sargent's instigation, we decided that rather than the sole target of our criticism being Fianna Fáil, we would instead level similar criticism at Fine Gael. On the following day, Trevor referred to Fine Gael as being 'Fianna Fáil-lite'. Fine Gael didn't react well to being attacked by the Greens to the extent that Fianna Fáil was. It obviously had an impact on relations between the parties in the post-election situation. On the whole, the change of tack probably made little material difference to Green support, but at least support levels seemed to be stabilising.

The more obvious reason for the dearth of support for the Mullingar Accord parties was the successful Fianna Fáil fight back, which was mainly being led by the Minister for Finance, Brian Cowen. His trenchant criticisms of opposition inconsistencies seemed to ring true with many voters, and were helping to turn the tide back in favour of Fianna Fáil.

The only leaders' debate of the campaign, limited to Bertie Ahern and Enda Kenny, wasn't thought likely to influence the election significantly. Neither was known for their oratorical skills. Both had to overcome significant negatives about themselves: Bertie Ahern had ongoing difficulties with the Mahon Tribunal; while Enda Kenny faced a widespread prejudice that he lacked credibility as an alternative Taoiseach. In the end, Bertie Ahern was seen to be the comprehensive winner of the debate, largely as a result of his having a better grasp of details.

This Bertie-versus-Enda theme was reinforced by a segment in *The Late Late Show* on RTÉ television on the final Friday before the end of the campaign. Three commentators: John Waters, Eoghan Harris and Eamon Dunphy, were lined up to give their views. The two-to-one verdict, given by Waters and Harris against Dunphy, proved to be a huge fillip to the Fianna Fáil recovery.

The other political parties were unhappy with the format that the broadcasting media, largely at the behest of RTÉ, had chosen for the leaders' debates. The main event was the head-to-head between the only acknowledged candidates to become Taoiseach. The other four party leaders were relegated to a likely Tánaiste debate. This preceded the Fianna Fáil/Fine Gael head-to-head.

Of the four participants in this debate, Trevor Sargent performed credibly. Michael McDowell secured debating points, if little else, with his quip that his opponents represented 'the left, the what's left and the leftovers'. Labour leader Pat Rabbitte disappointed, as he had also developed a reputation for a quick quip that wasn't much to the fore on this occasion. The real loser of the debate was Sinn Féin's Gerry Adams, not a candidate in the election, who showed himself to possess a very poor knowledge of economics.

In an extremely crowded media environment, the Greens did succeed in breaking through and making our presence felt a number of times in the campaign. Some political commentators attempted to define and create a fault line in the Green parliamentary party where none really existed. Trevor and John were the traditionalists. The 'modernisers' were called 'The Gonzaga Set' after the school that Eamon Ryan and Ciarán Cuffe had gone to, as did Michael McDowell. Apparently I was part of that set. I found the labelling annoying. While I got well with both Eamon and Ciarán, I hadn't gone to a fee-paying school. My father had been an islander who worked as a merchant seaman. I thought of myself as being quite a distance from being the middle-class Green stereotype with which some in the media felt comfortable. To me, it was another example of the media creating a narrative that didn't exist in reality.

On the other hand, our economic policy launch was well received, earning a welcoming article from Marc Coleman, then economics editor with *The Irish Times*:

> Radical you might say, controversial even. However you describe their manifesto, there is little doubt in the mind of this writer at least on one thing. For its cohesiveness and prudence, yesterday's Green Party manifesto was the most impressive in this campaign so far.
>
> Perhaps this should have been guessed, given where the presentation occurred - in the former Bank of Ireland building, now a restaurant, on Dublin's Dame Street, across the road from the Central Bank. There, dressed in neat banker suits, Trevor Sargent, Dan Boyle and Eamon Ryan set out their policies.
>
> As the main author and party finance spokesman, Dan Boyle, began talking, I thought I was attending a Department of Finance briefing when he explained why the Greens had taken more recent and lower forecasts for the economy as their benchmark for policy planning.

The analysis recognised much of what we were trying to achieve with our economic policies, even down to the fact of why we were presenting them where and how we were. The Bankers Bar and Restaurant in College Green with its affluent surrounds and fittings seemed the least likely setting for a Green Party policy launch. The location opposite the Central Bank headquarters was also a statement, as were the suits.

To be fair, one of the few points of division that existed in the Green parliamentary party in the 29th Dáil was the sartorial difference between Trevor Sargent, John Gormley and I, who were always fully suited up, and the others, who largely went without ties. For my part, my desire to blend in was informed by a quote I had once seen attributed to the murdered South African activist Stephen Biko, to the effect that if you wanted to say or do anything radical, wear a suit.

It was on the content of the policy that Marc Coleman's article was most in line with what we were trying to achieve. He quoted me as saying: 'The Irish economy has been inflated by some factors that may not exist in the medium term.' That was something about which I should probably have been more forthright. It was me saying, on behalf of the Green Party, that we didn't believe that the property boom, and what it was founded upon, could be sustained. Nor did we believe that economic growth would be relentless and continue well into the future. When it came to the Irish economy it was time for some black-sky thinking, but the larger political parties found it more convenient to tell peo-ple what they wanted to hear in exchange for their votes – a shared illusion that had somehow been mistaken for reality.

Subsequent revisionism would have us believe that other opposition parties were saying these things. They weren't. All produced election manifestos that signalled a continuing high rise in economic growth for several years to come. All contained policies designed to inflate the property boom even further. In a significant departure from their political stereotype, and in a very naked attempt to win over middle-class voters, the Labour Party was even proposing income tax cuts that would benefit higher earners!

What was different about what the Green Party was saying was that, while we foresaw a significant level of economic growth in the short term, such growth would be lower than what the other political parties believed was possible. We further believed that the rate of further growth would reduce, and that the factors that had brought about the rapid and widespread growth of the Irish economy in the previous ten years were not as real as they seemed. We were also to the fore in saying that proper control was needed over the public finances by restricting spending and increasing revenue. There was also the reference that the banks should contribute more to the running of the country through a new bank levy, although we weren't able to guess the scale of bank mismanagement that would be revealed later.

The closing paragraph of the article underlined that the Green Party's electoral strategy was focused on being available for whatever combination of parties would follow the general election result. That Coleman even included references to whether our economic policies would be acceptable to either Fianna Fáil or to Fine Gael revealed just how open our strategy was.

What we didn't do, and what Coleman's piece didn't pick up on, was highlight the more the essential difference between the Green approach to economics and that of the other political parties. As Greens, we question the value of what is presented as economic growth, and we reject the constant goal of achieving economic growth as being the keystone of economic policy. For Greens, how growth is defined is flawed as any economic activity, no matter how negative, is seen as contributing to economic growth.

For political reasons we chose not to emphasise this in the 2007 election. It was a silence brought about by a fear of being misrepresented. Our economic proposals promoting positive activities would create short-term economic growth. In the longer term, our commitment to sustainability meant that the constant utilising of depleting resources was not possible and shouldn't be the cornerstone of economic policy. For those whose support we sought, we believed that it was understood where the Greens stood on such issues.

Our general election manifesto also sought to get across this sense of balance and proportion. Carefully worded, it stressed difference. In places it was certainly radical, but not so radical, we thought, as to frighten the horses. Many commitments were not as emphasised or as prioritised as they were subsequently seen to be by others. For example, our policy positions on animal welfare were in the final paragraph of the environment section, itself several sections into the manifesto document. In this, we reiterated our opposition to blood sports, but we didn't state which blood sports we wished to see made illegal, or by when. We knew that progress on animal welfare issues would be difficult, and did not want to tie our hands prior to negotiations.

***

The other event in which the Greens were able to sneak into media prominence owed as much to personal constituency grievances as to electoral strategy. In what became known as the 'Rumble in Ranelagh', John Gormley faced up to Michael McDowell in a televised, on-street, political pitched battle.

There was no doubt that this was personal. Having first won a Dáil seat in 1987, McDowell lost that seat in the 1989 election, which was to be John Gormley's first general election. John did not win a seat, but had performed better than Michael McDowell, and had come close to winning the seat eventually won by Garrett FitzGerald. There is no doubt that McDowell saw John's good performance as a factor that damaged his attempt to retain the seat.

In 1992, McDowell won back a Dáil seat when John suffered from the effect of the Labour Spring Tide. It was in the 1997 general election that this antipathy reached its height. The Dublin South East count produced the narrowest result for a final seat in the country. Fighting it out for that last seat were the incumbent Michael McDowell and John Gormley, seeking to win a Dáil seat for the first time. Several days of recounting followed. John was ahead, and stayed ahead with his margin actually increasing, but that margin of 27 votes showed how close the electoral fortunes of these two were. The 2002 election saw the unique experience of both being elected. In 2007, both knew that it would be a case of it's either him or me regarding who would be a member of the 30th Dáil.

The meeting that led to the 'Rumble' was utterly accidental. John Gormley, who was around the precincts of Leinster House, struck up a conversation with Fionnan Sheehan, political reporter with the *Irish Independent*. During the conversation, Fionnan informed John that Michael McDowell's media event that day was to place a themed election poster on a street pole. This was to repeat a stroke that had worked so successfully for the Progressive Democrats in 2002 with the erection of the 'Single Party

Government – No Thanks' poster, this time with a 'Left Wing Government – No Thanks' message.

Mention of this lit a fuse in John. He went directly to where the event was meant to take place. He had had only twenty minutes' notice. When he got there, the media scrum was in place, taking photographs of PD Minister for State Liz O'Donnell half way up a ladder, but not actually putting up a poster. As she somewhat gracefully descended, Michael McDowell began to speak at the start of what he thought would be an off-the-cuff press conference.

Before he could get his first sentence out, he was interrupted by John Gormley. Having seen him, McDowell tried to make light of the situation by asking whether it was John Gormley or Michael Foot (a former British Labour Party leader, known for his constant wearing of an anorak). John held up a PD election leaflet saying: 'I have here one of your election booklets. In it you say we [the Greens] will increase corporation tax. That is a lie. Will you withdraw that?'

McDowell responded by asking his own question: 'Are you trying to introduce a €200 million levy on financial institutions?' This was true, but it wasn't a proposal to increase corporation tax. The conversation continued, becoming increasingly more heated, animated and passionate. John accused McDowell of using half-truths and misrepresenting the views of others, which had been his modus operandi.

McDowell responded with further questions – Does your party intend to introduce a property tax especially on second homes? The answer was no to the first part and yes to the second. Does your party want to reduce the tax relief on pensions? The answer was that we wanted to make the relief fairer.

And on it went. It was hardly edifying, but it was to be a major item on that evening's news. It fulfilled several purposes. It ensured that the last-week squeeze that had usually afflicted the Greens in elections was stemmed. John had defined his political battle as a Gormley versus McDowell fight to the death in Dublin South East. Most importantly, it gave Green activists great heart and encouragement for the final days of the campaign.

***

The final election results saw the Fianna Fáil recovery completed. Its vote marginally increased, but they lost one seat, which in reality was the seat won as an independent by Beverley Cooper Flynn in Mayo. Fine Gael recovered much of the lost ground they had suffered in 2002. Labour flatlined, losing one seat and winning only 10% of the national vote. Sinn Féin had only a marginal increase in their vote, but managed to lose one seat. Many of the independents who had been elected in 2002 failed to hold their seats.

The biggest election losers were the Progressive Democrats, who saw their seat total reduce from eight to two. Among their casualties was party leader Michael McDowell, who again lost to John Gormley, once again by a narrow margin. The scale of their losses brought into focus their very future as a political party.

Early on during count day it was being wondered whether the Greens would win any seats at all. The 4.7% of the national poll was slightly below the 5% target. We had an increase of slightly less than 1% nationally, but we had also run more candidates than we had in 2002. That meant that the vote on average actually fell in the constituencies where we had won seats in 2002.

In Cork South Central I felt this most acutely. In a larger poll, my vote was marginally down in percentage terms from

2002. In actual votes, it was seven votes fewer. It was enough in the end to make a difference. I had started that count day in a way that was becoming traditional for me. I visited my father's grave, walking four miles from my home to the cemetery in Mahon. From there, I crossed the River Lee across to Rochestown, back through Douglas to my house in Capwell, an eight-mile round trip.

By lunch-time I hadn't heard from any of my team at the count centre in Cork City Hall. I was preparing myself for the worst, but also thinking that they wanted to be sure before letting me know. When the call came, it wasn't as bad as I had feared. I was further down the polls than I needed to be, but, as in 2002, there was a considerable bunching of candidates, with five having no more than 600 votes between them on the first count. My problem was that there was a significant gap between me and the candidates ahead of me, while the amount of votes below me were far less than I needed to allow me to catch up.

I caught up and passed out Fine Gael's Jerry Buttimer. I was closing in on Labour's Ciarán Lynch. The 550-vote gap he had had on the first count had reduced to little more than 200 votes, but with Jerry Buttimer's transfer the gap increased again to 282 votes, half of 1% of the electorate. Those around me knew what had happened. The transfers prompted by the Mullingar Accord had sealed my fate. I had lost my seat.

I hadn't been helped by local opinion polls indicating that I would be safely elected, or by the bookmakers who had called the seat for me at ridiculous odds. Ivan Yates' Celtic Bookmakers were offering odds of 33 to 1 on; €1 won for every €33 put down. These unfounded and unhelpful opinions gave challengers the ability to knock on doors in the constituency and say that I didn't need the number-one vote as I would be comfortably elected. It became impossible to challenge.

Another, and perhaps more likely, reason was that I was perceived as not paying as much attention to my local role as I should have been. It was apparent during the campaign, and had been apparent during my term in Dáil Éireann, that I had been playing too much of a national role for some of my constituents. I don't believe that I did neglect my local role, but I do accept that I allowed it to be seen as if I was. This balance between the local and national is more striking in a smaller party. Back-benchers in more traditional parties can be totally anonymous at a national level so long as they are seen to be doing the right things locally. I was aware of the risk, and yet I still believe that the national role is more important. If given the opportunity to run that campaign again, there isn't much that I would do differently.

***

The question of whether or not I would be re-elected consumed much of my attention that day, but events in other constituencies also seemed very uncertain for the Greens. As the official first counts came in, the early pronouncements of doom for the Greens became less of a worry. Trevor Sargent, Eamon Ryan and Paul Gogarty would each be comfortably re-elected. Questions remained in all the other constituencies.

John Gormley was engaged in his seemingly perennial struggle with Michael McDowell in Dublin South East. Ciarán Cuffe was struggling in Dún Laoghaire after a strong performance from Richard Boyd Barrett of the Socialist Workers Party, operating under the collective *nom de plume* of 'People Before Profit'. Mary White in Carlow-Kilkenny was marginally down on her 2002 vote, but poor candidate selection by Fine Gael was giving her a chance to slip through. John saw off Michael McDowell again. Ciarán had less of a comfort zone over Richard Boyd Barrett, but the Fine Gael bungling allowed Mary White to make history and become the first female TD to be elected in that constituency.

Mary's election helped ease somewhat the pain of my own electoral failure. And her success, in a constituency with a large rural component, also seemed to augur well for the future.

There were other good performances that could have come off, but at least gave cause for further hope. Mark Dearey, running as a first-time candidate in Louth, performed very well. Déirdre de Búrca, standing as a second-time candidate in Wicklow, while never close to a seat still secured a vote comparable to mine, or Ciarán Cuffe's or Mary White's nonetheless.

Our other target seat in Galway West was a source of disappointment. Niall O'Brolchain had come into the election with a greatly enhanced local reputation (and something of a national reputation too) on his becoming Mayor of Galway. Ironically enough, this reputation was not to help positively in his favour in the general election.

In the immediate months coming up to the general election, Galway City and its environs were gripped by a water pollution crisis. The parasite cryptosporidium had entered the city's drinking-water supplies, with upwards of 200 people becoming infected with cryptosporidiosis. In his public statements as mayor, Niall O'Brolchain defended Galway City Council officials, whose previous actions (or lack thereof) were a key component of this crisis coming about. This defence did not inspire public confidence, or do anything to solidify public support.

In the end, winning six seats nationally seemed a satisfactory outcome for the Greens. After all, with the exceptions of Fianna Fáil and Fine Gael, all other political groupings had gone backwards. What the election results also showed, however, was an inherent weakness in Green Party support; a weakness that wouldn't withstand the negative impact upon support that going into government and making decisions in government would bring about.

Perhaps the most telling example of where the Green Party was at this point could be seen from a publicity photograph from the election campaign. In seeking to highlight our commitment to bring more women in public life, five of our female candidates posed for a photo. Two of the candidates: Mary White standing in Carlow/Kilkenny, and Elizabeth Davidson, a candidate in Dublin South West, were to continue to play high-level roles in the running of the party. The other three women: Patricia McKenna, Bronwen Maher and Déirdre de Búrca, would soon each personify many of the difficulties that lay ahead.

3 | Playing Senior Hurling Now

The electoral arithmetic in the aftermath of the general election virtually guaranteed Bertie Ahern's re-election as Taoiseach. 77 Fianna Fáil seats, added to the two remaining Progressive Democrats (Mary Harney and Noel Grealish), added to two Fianna Fáil 'gene pool[1]' independents in the form of Jackie Healy Rae and Beverley Flynn brought him to 81 of the 83 votes he needed. Fianna Fáil sources were briefing political journalists that Finian McGrath could be brought into the fold. The same sources were suggesting that, surprisingly, Michael Lowry, the former Fine Gael TD, could also be seen as a like-minded independent and support Ahern. Knitting together this type of support would undoubtedly bring Ahern back again into Government Buildings as Taoiseach, but no guarantee existed regarding the long-term stability of a government formed in this way.

What seemed less likely were the suggestions that longstanding independent Tony Gregory could be brought into this arrangement, or possibly be offered the position of Ceann Comhairle. Most Leinster House insiders discounted these suggestions, as the ongoing antipathy between the two Dublin Central colleagues, Ahern and Gregory, was long known and understood. Gregory's office and mine were

---

[1] As the former Fianna Fáil TDs had come to be known in public discussions of the Dáil arithmetic.

close to each other in Leinster House. We were also whips in our respective groupings. I found that his more personal knowledge of Ahern, and his advice, were always helpful.

His immediate pronouncements indicated that Ahern had yet to consider a Labour or Green Party option. We took such statements with a grain of salt. It had been clear that considerable love-bombing of the Greens had been undertaken by Fianna Fáil and Ahern during the course of the general election. It seemed to us that huge measures were being put in place to move Fianna Fáil away from its previously antipathetic position towards the Greens, best exemplified by John O'Donoghue's phlegmatic retort that 'Ireland needs the Greens like a lettuce needs a slug'.

Well in advance of the general election, nodding and winking was afoot. Seamus Brennan, the Mr Nice of Fianna Fáil, was the person designated to make contact. He performed what many had considered were political miracles when he was the government Chief Whip in the 1997-2002 minority administration. During that period, John Gormley and he served together on the Party Whips' group, where they struck up a good personal relationship. 'Don't rule us out, John', Seamus Brennan would regularly say to John in early 2007, well aware of the mood music coming out from the Greens, particularly from our party conference.

On the Sunday after the general election, Seamus Brennan made his first informal approach to John Gormley. It was along the lines of 'would we be interested in participating in talks on the formation of a government?' John brought this back to the parliamentary party and other groupings within the party and it was tentatively agreed to proceed.

None of this was happening at breakneck speed. The informal approach was a couple of days after the counting of votes in the election had finished. There then followed a couple of days' consultation within the Green Party, and this was all in advance of any formal approach being made. The election was held on May 24th, with the Dáil set to return on June 13th. There was little time for negotiation.

In the meantime, the Green Party had prepared for any possible negotiations as best we could, still not knowing with whom we would be negotiating, or when. Before the election we had established a putative negotiating team that consisted of John Gormley as Party Chair, Donal Geoghegan as Party General Secretary and myself as Party Whip.

My failure to be elected introduced a note of uncertainty as to whether I would be involved in this process at all. At a meeting on the Tuesday after the general election, Trevor Sargent told me he very much wanted me to be involved. I was grateful for his confidence. He wanted me to be considered a virtual and a continuing member of the parliamentary party.

My sense of that meeting was that it was an extremely personal occasion. Trevor would have been aware that my confidence had been shot. By way of seeking to empathise, he made me aware of difficult things happening in his life. His marriage had broken down, and few were aware of this. He also confided in me that he would be following through on his intention to live up to his general election statement that he would resign as party leader should the party be going into government with Fianna Fáil. That was something he had yet to affirm with anyone else. My respect for Trevor, always high, deepened as a result of that meeting.

I still had my reservations. I had not been elected. I was not a party official. At best I was an interim party official, until whatever process that was going to proceed had finished. I knew that there would be some, although not many, in the party who would be unhappy that I would be involved in this process at all. It also, I feared, offered more political hostages to fortune. Despite those misgivings, I wanted to be involved.

A full week had passed since the holding of the general election, and still there was no indication as to the likely start of talks. Increasingly, the expectation was that talks with Fianna Fáil were imminent. Despite this probability, it did not preclude keeping options on any possible alternative government. Even at that stage, that was our preferred option. To this end, contact was maintained with Fine Gael, with Phil Hogan being their main contact. Communications with Fine Gael were confused to say the least, and ranged from the badgering to the pleading.

Dark mutterings about the contents of the Mahon Tribunal's investigations on Bertie Ahern were commonplace, but made more as threats than advice. The main stumbling block, however, was the issue of whether the numbers could be made to add up. We believed that they could, and cited the 'everyone but Fianna Fáil' government of 1948 as a precedent. David McCullagh, RTÉ's political correspondent, had written an excellent book on the experiences of that government. That government, I felt, could be used as a template for any government likely to be formed under similar circumstances.

In 1948, as in 2007, it seemed unlikely that political parties could come together. It wasn't without complications. The Progressive Democrats had stated they would not serve in a government with the Labour Party, although that was seen as posturing by many. Sinn Féin remained political pariahs with all political parties except the Greens, ruling them out as potential partners in government, even though some seemed more willing to examine the prospect than others.

Fine Gael found the concept extremely difficult to come around to. We felt that, as the largest party in any alternative government, they had an obligation to talk directly to Sinn Féin. Fine Gael was most reluctant to do this. Eventually word came back to us through Phil Hogan that Fine Gael leader Enda Kenny wanted the Greens to act as a proxy in approaching Sinn Féin. This was confirmed in a subsequent phone conversation that took place between Trevor Sargent and Enda Kenny. The existence of exchanges was subsequently denied by Fine Gael, which led to considerable distrust between our parties, and especially between the Greens and the principal actors within Fine Gael.

Even if the numbers could be made to add up, as a party we didn't feel that negotiations with Fine Gael would be any easier or any different than they would be with Fianna Fáil. We Greens have never seen any policy differences between Fianna Fáil and Fine Gael, and any cultural differences were slight, offering little in the way of positive choice.

John Gormley tells the story of being canvassed a long time previously by Fine Gael activists. 'Can you tell me what the policy differences are between Fine Gael and Fianna Fáil?' he asked. After something of a pause the answer he got was: 'I suppose there aren't any, but I think you'll find that in Fine Gael you find a better class of person.'

It was to prove academic in any case, as the two Progressive Democrat TDs seemed unlikely to remove themselves from their existing coalition choice. Within the Green Party, informal consultations with members were continuing. Members of the parliamentary party sought to attend as many local group meetings as possible to gauge the mood within the party. On June 1st I attended one such meeting in Wicklow. It was well attended, and it reflected a general feeling that as a party we should proceed to negotiations for government.

As the preferred alternative government option receded, the formal approach from Fianna Fáil finally came and was accepted. Talks began on Sunday June 3rd. That was ten days after the general election, and only ten days from when the Dáil was meant to reconvene. Sunday was a strange day on which to begin negotiations, but time was shortening. It felt surreal, as a negotiating team, to be walking along Merrion Street that morning. As John Gormley, Donal Geoghegan and I approached the gates of Government Buildings, we were met by a large media scrum. While we should have anticipated some media interest, none of us expected the scale of the media presence, which remained in place throughout the negotiations.

John did the talking while Donal and I nodded in unison. The preliminaries out of the way, we continued through to the doors of Government Buildings. After coming through the media barrage, none of us were intimidated by the rest of this journey. Government Buildings held little mystique for us: over the years, Donal and I had attended meetings regularly with the National Economic and Social Council in the Italian Room there. Even though he now had ten years' Leinster House experience behind him, John would have visited Government Buildings less often, but it wasn't a novel experience for him either.

The negotiations took place more around than in Government Buildings. Most of the talking was to be in Seamus Brennan's office in the ministerial corridor, located in the link between Leinster House and Government Buildings. Brennan was the outgoing Minister for Social and Family Affairs. Other offices in the ministerial corridor were made available for other uses. One office was for the use of the

Green Party backup team of Carol Fox, Aoife Ni Lochlainn and Sue Duke. Another office was a neutral space for teas/ sandwiches and many, many cakes – designed, no doubt, to keep us sweet.

Watching television on the night before the talks began, I caught an episode of RTÉ's archives programme *Reeling In The Years*. 1992 was the theme of that night's episode. One item was the opening of programme for government negotiations between Fianna Fáil and The Labour Party. The Fianna Fáil team consisted of Brian Cowen, Noel Dempsey and Mary O'Rourke. Fifteen years later, after several more negotiations on programmes for government, it was largely the same team. We were up against negotiators of proven experience in an environment where the odds were already heavily stacked against us.

That experience translated into each of the Fianna Fáil negotiating team having a defined role. Things were less clear-cut within the Green negotiating team. As first-time negotiators, slotting into psychologically defined roles was not particularly high on our agenda. I suppose that I was the closest to being the bad cop, although John Gormley let his agitation be known throughout the talks. Donal Geoghegan was more cool and reasoned, teasing out policy nuances.

When the talking finally started, Seamus Brennan made what has become his infamous remark: 'Lads, you're play- ing senior hurling now.' It was said half-heartedly, but it was clear that there was also an intent there. The implication was Fianna Fáil were the big boys, the practiced survivors, and that we were there half under sufferance.

This attitude continued through to the first substan- tial policy discussion on the economy. Brian Cowen made it quite clear that the economic projections contained in the Fianna Fáil/Progressive Democrat joint election programme were the figures that would be adhered to. 'Fine,' I said, 'they're wrong.' I knew that these projections were a huge fiction that would have to be adjusted at the first budget.

Maybe failing to challenge those figures was a mistake. Department of Finance projections were rarely accurate. In boom years, that didn't seem to matter. The estimates and the budget always adjusted the poor projections that preceded them. This laxity in the importance of proper fore-casting was as strong a failing in the civil service as it was in the political system, and would be a key factor in what was to happen subsequently.

The elephant in the room during these negotia-tions was the Progressive Democrats. As far as we were concerned, this was a negotiation between the Green Party and Fianna Fáil. We were not negotiating with the Progressive Democrats, and did not want to negotiate with the Progressive Democrats. Between us, Fianna Fáil and the Greens had eighty-four seats: a Dáil majority. If other parties wanted to support the government and to strengthen the majority, then that was a matter for them.

The first day of the negotiations was as much about what was not being said as it was about what was being positively agreed. The areas of disagreement, of which there were many, including taxation and economic policy; roads funding versus public transport; co-location of private hos-pitals on public land; carbon emissions targets and levies; planning and housing; a ban on corporate donations and Shannon Airport's use by the US military were parked to one side while efforts were made to find levels of agree-ment in other policy areas.

Our first error was the use of the Fianna Fáil election manifesto as a source document. It was our intention to open both manifestos and subsequently produce a new document.

No agreement was ever sought or reached that the Fianna Fáil manifesto should be the source document. It was later to become an area of contention during the negotiations.

A secondary series of problems quickly became prominent. Not only were we negotiating with a proven team of negotiators, behind and parallel to them was the civil service. While anything might be possible, the civil service frustrated us by saying that certain things would be difficult, or that parts of the Green manifesto were not technically or legally possible. This was an experience to which we became inured.

The atmosphere of the opening few days of the talks was workmanlike. Seamus Brennan played the cordial host with consummate ease, Noel Dempsey engaged on all the policy issues, while Brian Cowen was more inscrutable. He was almost surly, and gave the impression that the talks were not his preferred option. Cowen gave every impression of being the loyal party member and doing his leader's bidding. While it was never stated, the impression existed that he would have much preferred to be negotiating with the Labour Party.

Tea breaks and sandwiches saw some small talk, but largely both delegations, when not engaged in talks with each other, kept to themselves by going to their own rooms. I can only remember one formal, catered lunch where I tried to have an informal conversation with Brian Cowen. I chose the subject of Offaly hurling, figuring it was a safe subject, but soon discovered that it was a theme that at that time was greatly depressing him. That said, he did loosen up somewhat and managed to tell some interesting and often humorous stories, especially about his period as Minister for Foreign Affairs. However, that was as intimate as relations got.

Progress, such as it was, on the first two days of the talks was turgidly slow. By Tuesday, the third day, John Gormley had taken to entering through the Leinster House entrance, leaving me to deal with the media. I didn't mind, as I found dealing with the media and the experience of being involved in the talks to be very therapeutic. At least I didn't have to dwell on my personal election result.

Because I hadn't been elected, I chose a relaxed, informal, even wisecracking approach to media enquiries, while doing my best to say little or nothing. In truth, as nothing was being agreed, I really didn't have anything to say. There were so many audiences that had to be addressed – Green Party members, Green Party supporters, Fianna Fáil and other political parties, and most importantly the general public itself. The important message to get out there was that the Greens were a party interested in being in government, and able to be responsible once there.

Throughout our political history we had battled with the perception, the often imposed perception, that we were flaky and not up to the business of government. It was a perception that we have found to be almost impossible to discard, with the myth holding a greater sway than truth or experience on the public consciousness. Nevertheless, during the period of talks at least, it was a myth that we were able temporarily to put to rest.

One of the greater culture shocks between the Fianna Fáil and Green negotiators was our consultation methods between talk sessions. While the Fianna Fáil negotiators weren't exactly plenipotentiaries, they did only have to consult with one person: Bertie Ahern. We Greens referred several times daily to a fifteen to twenty person reference group waiting for us at our party headquarters on Suffolk Street.

The reference group was made up of the Green parliamentary party, members of the party's national executive, the

chair of our National Council and designated local government representatives. The views of that group represented all
views that were found in the party. The reference group was
particularly of the view, which was predominant in the party,
that Fianna Fáil was far from being our preferred partner in
government. Despite this natural inclination, throughout the
days and days of detailed meetings, not one leak from the
programme for government emanated from this group. For
some, this indicated a maturity and sense of responsibility
that hadn't previously been associated with the Green Party.
Senior Greens were also nervous and looking for information. Déirdre de Búrca, away on a sun holiday with her family,
constantly sent texts independently to each of the Green
negotiators wanting to know what was happening.

From the outset, the talks with Fianna Fáil were a hard
sell for our reference group. While John, Donal and I tried to
eke out what we could from the Fianna Fáil team, the reference group was going through the various permutations to
see what was possible and what the red-line issues were.
In Suffolk Street, Ciarán Cuffe became that man with the
flip chart, writing and rewriting what the issues were, what
had been offered and what was needed to report progress.
On days one and two, the reference group was far from
impressed with what was being offered.

By day three, Tuesday, John Gormley wasn't impressed
either. John had found the talks process hugely frustrating.
He would regularly leave his seat at the talks table and walk
agitatedly in the nearby corridor. On that day he got very
pushy on the subject of gay marriage. While gay marriage
was Green Party policy, our election manifesto committed
us to achieving civil partnership as a first step in this process.
Civil Partnership was also in the Fianna Fáil manifesto, but we
did not believe that they, or indeed Fine Gael, would really

implement such legislation. John wanted to test to what extent they were committed to this goal by seeing how far they would go towards bringing gay marriage about. Not far. I suspect that John didn't expect them to, and wanted them to react as they did so that he could propose what he was to propose at that evening's meeting with the reference group.

As head of the delegation, John spoke first. He made it quite clear that he felt that the talks were not going anywhere and that the time had come to bring them to an end. Donal Geoghegan and I looked at each other, somewhat amazed. We were aware of his unhappiness, but despite having spent all day with each other at the negotiations, we had not had a review meeting at the end of the day prior to meeting with the reference group. We had not agreed together to make a recommendation to quit the talks.

John had made a pre-emptive strike. The thought was firmly planted in the minds of the reference group members. Donal and I had to summon up all of our persuasive abilities to outline why we needed to carry on. Our main arguments were that to leave talks so early in the process would reflect badly on the party. The beginning of any set of negotiations was a feeling out, softening-up process. Agreement and gains invariably came towards the end of such a process. 'Nothing was agreed until everything was agreed' had been our mantra.

We stated our fear that early ending of the talks would lead to Fianna Fáil inspired leaks that talks had broken down on the issue of gay marriage, and that we weren't serious about the wider policy agenda. It was a close call, but we somehow managed to convince the reference group that we should proceed, which John also accepted. If the talks had collapsed then I'm certain they would not have resumed.

On the following day, Wednesday, after the previous evening's fraught reference group meeting, the Green negotiators agreed to take a harder line in the talks. That morning I got especially angry with Brian Cowen. I asked him what the Greens had been given in the way of concessions since the talks had started.

'There's a lot we've given way on,' Cowen said.

'Like?' I asked. The Fianna Fáil negotiators looked at each other, unable to respond.

The display of petulance and aggression seemed to reap some dividends. There began to be some give on the Fianna Fáil side, although nothing on the substantive issues. That afternoon, Eamon Ryan came and engaged in one-to-one negotiations with Noel Dempsey, with a particular emphasis on energy policy. They were very productive talks that resulted in agreement on several measures that had an identifiable green print in the eventual programme for government.

It was to be a false dawn. On Thursday, the Green negotiating team felt no progress was being made on the substantive issues. We further decided that, if there was no change on the following day, Friday, we would collectively recommend pulling out of the talks.

There was no change on Friday. The Green negotiators went to the reference group and said that the talks should end. There would be a possibility that they could resume, but we were ending these talks without any expectation that they would. The reference group unanimously accepted the recommendation. The hope had been that if agreement could be reached then a special members' convention would be held on the following day at the Mansion House. The decision to withdraw from talks well and truly scuppered those plans. A weekend date was thought best in achieving maximum participation of our members, but this would now not be possible.

As we were leaving Suffolk Street to return to Government Buildings to inform the Fianna Fáil team, Donal Geoghegan turned to me and said: 'We've fucked it up.'

'No,' I replied, 'they'll come back to us again.'

The formal ending of the talks was muted. We each thanked each other for having listened to our respective cases, and then went on our way. The three Greens were on our way to the Shelbourne Hotel, where we had arranged a press conference.

While we were getting ready for the press conference, an *Irish Times* photographer took a photograph of me with my head in my hands, sitting next to John Gormley, who was scratching his. I suppose that this was meant to depict the stress of the situation, but in my case I had been out the previous evening with Ciarán Cuffe and some other friends, and my temples were still not restored to their natural state.

The press conference itself saw a media that was sympathetic to the situation. There seemed to be surprise that we withdrew from the talks. The questioning was brief, and the conference finished quite quickly. Part of the reason was that the RTÉ's *Six One News* wanted to conduct a live interview by Charlie Bird with Trevor and me. When asked why I believed that the talks had failed, I said that there was little that had been achieved in which our party members could take pride.

Within ten minutes of that interview, I received a call on my mobile phone from Noel Dempsey, who thanked me for not taking the opportunity to load the blame for the talks collapsing onto Fianna Fáil's shoulders. In the same hour, Seamus Brennan had made a similar phone call to John Gormley.

I walked with Paul Gogarty from the Shelbourne back to Suffolk Street for a review meeting with the reference group. I received a text. It was from my Mother. 'Never mind we still love you', it said. I have to admit that I started to choke up. 'Are you having an asthma attack?' he asked. That certainly helped me to regain my composure.

***

Throughout the talks, various other senior members of Fianna Fáil sought to open communication channels. This continued throughout the period following the collapse of the talks. Donal Geoghegan received calls from his Fianna Fáil counterpart, Sean Dorgan. I was getting calls from Micheál Martin. While Micheál and I had shared a long history together, we had never been particularly close. I was more than a little surprised to get these calls. It's hard to know whether these calls were being made as part of any co-ordinated strategy on Fianna Fáil's part, or whether they were more a matter of attempts by the individuals concerned to be part of the process. Whatever the motivation, the calls continued, each seeking to resuscitate the talks. John Gormley and Seamus Brennan were in back-and-forth contact throughout the weekend with nothing new forthcoming.

On Sunday, nothing new seemed to happen either until later that evening, when Seamus Brennan and I appeared on that week's edition of *The Week in Politics* on RTÉ 1. The programme was recorded at the RTÉ studios in Donnybrook, but I was being filmed from the RTÉ studios in Cork. This added to the surreal nature of the programme. Presenter Sean O'Rourke sat with other panel members, while Seamus Brennan and I conducted a bizarre on-screen negotiation.

I travelled to Dublin on the first train on Monday morning, not knowing whether talks were going to recommence or not. Reopening talks would not be easy. 48 hours was all the time that was available to start talks, reach agreement and organise a members' conference, but we still hoped that something could be made to happen. By the time I had arrived, we had received another document from Fianna Fáil, which conceded ground on some of the areas where obstacles existed. On presenting this document to our reference group, it was felt that a basis to restart the talks was there. That afternoon, and late into the evening, the two negotiation teams worked to dot 'i's and cross 't's

While the talks were going on, the Green background team were working on an alternative draft. It was important to us that any agreed programme of government did not read like a recently presented general election manifesto. The new draft didn't include any new material, but we felt that it would read better.

On Tuesday morning in the reception room of the Taoiseach's offices in Government Buildings, I presented the new draft to Gerry Hickey, programme manager to Bertie Ahern and Brian Murphy, who also worked in his office. They were aghast. It was too late to present a new draft, they claimed. Possibly it was, but that meant that we had lost control of the script, and the original mistake of using Fianna Fáil's election manifesto as a template would be compounded. It was another valuable lesson learned.

From there on in, the negotiating teams were stood down. It was left for Noel Dempsey and I to agree final areas and arrange the draft programme, prior to it being presented and recommended to the Green Party's reference group. Insertions were put in. The order of sections was changed. While the draft was substantially based around the Fianna Fáil election manifesto, there were, however, some significant differences.

The programme's commitments on energy were all new, and all came from the Green Party. The justice section was also substantially changed. The failure of Michael McDowell to be re-elected saw no one willing to fight for many of the previous commitments being included. As a more liberal party, that suited the Greens down to the ground. On the Greens' behalf, a great deal of the work in having new commitments included in this area was successfully done by Niamh Allen, a parliamentary researcher for Ciarán Cuffe, who had established good contacts with NGOs, especially relating to reform.

The initial criticism of the environment section was that it coincided too closely to what was originally in the Fianna Fáil manifesto. We didn't have a great deal of difficulty with that. We knew that in the run up to the election Fianna Fáil had met with all the main environmental NGOs. The manifesto regurgitated their wish lists. We had experience of previous unsatisfied manifesto commitments. We cynically believed that, without Green involvement in government, these commitments would never see the light of day.

Taxation remained a bugbear. We wanted a recasting of the taxation system to reduce and then remove the unhealthy emphasis on property-based forms of tax relief; a reliance that we felt would come to haunt the country. We secured no commitments on this, but we did propose and have accepted the need to establish a Commission on Taxation. This was obviously a half-a-loaf approach; however, we believed that such a commission could have had the impact that a previous commission had had in the early 1980s.

What was probably most difficult for us was the insistence of Fianna Fáil that Mary Harney and what was left of the Progressive Democrats should continue as part of the incoming government. Throughout the talks we tried each angle – no Progressive Democrats, no Mary Harney, no further involvement at the Department of Health – but were beaten back each time by Fianna Fáil. While it was never directly said, Mary Harney at the Department of Health provided convenient political cover for Fianna Fáil; a useful buffer zone from the regularly unpopular decisions that came from that department.

We never negotiated with the Progressive Democrats, nor did we see them as part of the process. We were aware, however, of Fianna Fáil negotiating for the Progressive Democrats on particular issues. This was especially true of the issue of co-located hospitals. We believed that co-located hospitals were a social and an economic nonsense. Brian Cowen argued strongly for them, claiming that they would free up more public beds. The closest to we got to a shared understanding on this was that, while not publicly stated, of the eight proposed hospitals, only two were strongly progressing, two were very unlikely to happen and the other four were unlikely to happen. We satisfied ourselves that, if in government, we would not support any measures designed to make any these additional hospitals more likely.

We adopted a similar approach to any agreement that Fianna Fáil sought to have with independent TDs who were willing to support a new government. We were not negotiating with them, and did not consider ourselves bound by any agreement reached between them and Fianna Fáil. During the talks, Seamus Brennan, who had been the Government Chief Whip charged with keeping several independent TDs toeing the line during the life of the 1997-2002 government, explained that this process was in any case overblown. His approach was to trawl through lists of already agreed infra-structural works, and then offer the government-supporting independent TDs the opportunity to make these announce-ments for their constituencies.

Parallel to discussions of completing the policy sections of the programme of government, the first meeting between Bertie Ahern and Trevor Sargent on the political framework of the likely government took place. This was to agree the number of Cabinet positions, the departments to be allo-cated, the number of junior ministries and the number of Seanad positions.

Trevor travelled to St Luke's in Drumcondra, the heart of Ahern's power base to conduct these talks. Our posi-tion was two Cabinet ministries, two junior ministries and three Seanad positions. We had no interest in the position of Tánaiste.

The talks went quite well. Trevor achieved more than I thought could be achieved. Bertie Ahern's original pitch was for one Cabinet position, with two junior ministries and one Seanad seat. As regards the Seanad, his and Fianna Fáil's argument was 'Don't worry, we'll look after Dan Boyle'. This type of thinking exemplified the cultural difference between the two parties. Being 'looked after' would never have been a motivation for us, but the need to have representation in the second chamber overseeing legislation in an agreed programme of government would have been.

In the end, Trevor secured two Cabinet positions, one junior ministry with a second to be added midway through the life of the government, and two Seanad seats. With simi-lar numbers in the previous government, the Progressive Democrats had secured four Seanad seats. We were satis-fied with two seats. That represented critical mass, and that was what was required.

Trevor also secured agreement on a list of infrastructural works to be undertaken during the life of the government. The parliamentary party was pleased with what Trevor had achieved. The process of agreeing it brought about a discussion between us on who would serve when during the life of the government; a discussion that would subsequently come back to haunt us.

In advance of the election, John Gormley had worried as to how we would decide who would take which ministerial position should we find ourselves in such a situation. Seniority was the obvious criterion. While it had never been said, the expectation was that Trevor and John would be Cabinet members. Eamon and I had expectations as a result of the increased profiles that we had developed during the previous Dáil.

My failure to be elected, and Trevor's position on being in government with Fianna Fáil, put John and Eamon into pole position. Ciarán Cuffe felt that he too should be considered. He had been elected to local government on the same day as Trevor, John and I had been. It was agreed that halfway through the life of a government, with a Cabinet reshuffle, Ciarán should be considered for a Cabinet position.

Trevor, who as leader was seeking to achieve an understanding on the issue, indicated that in accepting a junior position he would be prepared to serve only for the first half of the government term. As the only female member of the parliamentary party, it was thought that Mary White would be put forward to be made a Minister of State during the life of the government.

In the event of the Greens getting a third junior ministry, Paul Gogarty would be a Minister of State for three years. I would have the opportunity of serving for two years. This was something with which I was quite happy to agree, as I never considered it likely to happen. As with so much of what we were talking about here, it would be couched by ifs and buts and situations that could never be foreseen, or so we thought.

This almost all became irrelevant. At Government Buildings I was finishing talks with Noel Dempsey when we came up against a huge obstacle: the ratio of spending between public transport and roads expenditure. We had a massive argument, the biggest that had taken place during the previous ten days. This was two hours before the final Green Party reference group meeting where they would approve or not approve this draft programme. I found it hard to agree to what was being proposed. I checked with Eamon Ryan, who was spokesperson for this area. He wasn't prepared to have the talks collapse on this issue, and reluctantly, I agreed. I felt that transport policy was an important area for the Greens, but had deferred to Eamon's opinion as spokesperson in the area that he wouldn't fight for that.

The reference group now had a full package before it. It would be fair to say that no one in the reference group was satisfied with what was agreed in policy terms. It was the Cabinet positions and the influence that could be had in government that proved to be the main selling point. Our expectations in policy terms, and our perceived bargaining leverage, were already in the lower range. Being in government and dealing with issues as they arose in government would be where we could exert worthwhile influence.

Alison Martin, the party's administrator, had prepared a digest for members of phone calls and emails that had come in from party members, supporters and members of the general public on the question of whether the Greens should enter into government or not. They were running two to one in favour of making the leap. It helped to concentrate minds.

The Members' Convention was held that evening at the Mansion House. The venue was chosen for many reasons. Being central, and close to Leinster House, it was chosen as much for its historical resonances as anything else. As the site of the first sitting of the first Dáil in 1919, it allowed us to mark our coming of age as a political party, and to write another chapter, albeit a small one, in Irish political history. It had been hoped to hold this meeting on the previous Saturday, but circumstances worked against that. Some members obviously were missing, however at over 700 people it was the largest and most representative gathering of Irish Greens ever held.

Outside, the usual suspects organised small protests. The 'not good enough' brigade wanted to make their presence felt. Richard Boyd Barrett and his Socialist Workers Party, armed with his megaphone, magnified their volume and their sense of outrage. Not far behind was Vincent Salafia, self-appointed guardian of Tara, spitting betrayal. Green Party members politely accepted whatever literature was offered and went on to enter the hall.

Before the main meeting began, a series of smaller meetings took place. Green Party local government representatives were learning for the first time the contents of the programme for government. They wanted to know to what extent they were expected to co-operate with Fianna Fáil, something that most councillors by inclination were not happy about. At local council level no such co-operation would be required. There was, though, an expectation that Fianna Fáil candidates would have to be voted for in the upcoming Seanad elections. This did not please many Green councillors. We rationalised the action as part of the process of government. In the Seanad elections the government had to collectively use its voting strength. A strong government majority in the Seanad was important. Fianna Fáil would be the beneficiaries, winning at least another two Seanad seats.

Meeting and mingling with party members before we started, I was overwhelmed by the goodwill that I was receiving. I felt that I had let people down by failing to get re-elected. This seemed to disappear as people expressed gratitude for work done during the negotiations. It also helped to sell several more copies of the party history book, which I was signing throughout the evening. One copy was proffered to me by two Wexford members, Niamh FitzGibbon who was with the youngest party member there that evening, 17-year-old Ciarán Lyng.

As regards getting the required result, Green Party conventions are impossible to manage. While speakers are required to apply for the right to speak, identifying where they stand beforehand on the motion being debated, speakers are then drawn by lot. Under this method, several members of the parliamentary party did not get to speak. Those who declared to speak were in favour of going into government by a ratio of two to one. As the party was required to pass the motion by a two-thirds majority this did not leave any room for complacency.

As Party Chair, John Gormley got to speak, as did Trevor Sargent as party leader. When Trevor mentioned that two Cabinet positions would be coming, it seemed to surprise many, but also helped to sway some members. Patricia McKenna made a passionate speech, as was her wont, arguing that it was too soon for the party to enter government.

I was given the job of selling the programme for government. I wasn't going to oversell it. Summoning up my best inner Eamon Dunphy I said that the programme wasn't a great document – it may not even have been a good document – but it had good within it, and that good had come from the Green Party. That seemed good enough for most of the members. I went on to say that going into government would see the party and its members experience many difficult events and choices, the like of which we had never experienced before. I certainly undersold that.

As we waited for the result to be announced, few of us knew what to expect. When it was announced that 84% of those present supported the programme for government and wanted the party to enter government, there was as much disbelief as there was delight. We were on our way. The emotion of the occasion got to many.

Trevor spoke to the meeting immediately upon the result being announced. He expressed his pride in the decision that the party had taken, and stressed the extent of the challenge it now faced. He went on to confirm what no one had expected of him: that he felt honour bound to step down as party leader. There was a stunned reaction. Trevor had made himself the Moses of the Green Party; often being the sole focal point for the party in its wilderness years. Now, at the moment of supposed triumph, he would not be sitting at the top table. While no one wanted him to take this course of action, all agreed that it was the mark of the man.

Despite the euphoria, I was feeling deflated. Part of this was exhaustion. Part of it was a realisation of how difficult the path we had chosen was likely to be.

The kissing and the embracing meant that it took a while for the hall to be emptied. Most of us repaired to Café en Seine across the road. I was met at the door by Sue Duke, who worked with Eamon Ryan, and who had become a good friend. We hugged – a hug that seemed to go on for minutes. It was the first of many other embraces that evening.

It was an embrace of another type later in that pub that gave me pause for thought. On a visit to the toilet, I met with Joe Burke, a member of Bertie Ahern's kitchen Cabinet. He outstretched his hand, and with his best 'hail fellow well met' said: 'welcome on board, Dan'. On the surface there wasn't much to take offence at, but as I heard that greeting it gave a meaning to the term 'on board' that I was meant to fully understand.

The new government would not begin its life until the following day, and already I was having doubts.

4 | A New Regime?

I had mixed feelings about the first day of the new Dáil. I had regrets that I wasn't a part of it; regrets added to a realisation that I would have had legitimate expectations of being part of the new Cabinet if I had been a part of it. There were several media requests, most of which I was happy to accept as a distraction from other events.

On the RTÉ television *News at One* I did an outside broadcast, speaking to newscaster Eileen Dunne in the studio. There, on a panel, was the Labour Party's Pat Magnier. In that peculiar Cork way he heaped praise on me, saying that I was the man who had put the government together. I wasn't taking any of that. 'I think you're building me up, Pat, so I'll be the one who takes the blame when it all goes wrong,' I said.

That afternoon I spent over two hours in a radio studio for the *Drivetime* programme as nominations were taken for the positions of Ceann Comharile and for Taoiseach. I went into Leinster House as the Dáil was reconvening for the announcement of the new Cabinet. I joined the crew of Green workers in Paul Gogarty's office. There was a carnival mood at play. I continued to feel wistful and a little sorry for myself, but like others felt no small pride when John Gormley and Eamon Ryan took their place on the Government front bench.

The Dáil debate on the formation of the new government saw Pat Rabbitte as leader of the Labour Party quote directly and extensively from what I had said to our party convention on the previous night. It was meant to be a closed meeting, but much of the proceedings were texted with abandon.

The debate was 'politics as usual', although in private some opposition TDs spoke more kindly. Later on that day I was taken aside in a corridor in Leinster House by Michael D. Higgins. With that innate decency of his, he wished us well on our journey in government. He went on to tell me how much he regretted that the Fianna Fáil/Labour government had disintegrated in 1994. His view was that Labour should have continued in government with Fianna Fáil after the Harry Whelehan affair had been overcome, that Labour was achieving much in government and that it would have achieved more had it remained in power.

Meanwhile, the choreography of coming into the Dáil chamber saw the protocol of Cabinet seniority place members of the Cabinet on the bench in order according to the length of their Cabinet experience. This saw John and Eamon being two of the three back markers. There was only one new Cabinet member from Fianna Fáil: Brian Lenihan as Minister for Justice. While this was a good appointment, many felt that the opportunity to radically refresh the Cabinet was being missed once again.

The Cabinet was modified to a very minimal extent. John O'Donoghue, who had been the most trenchant critic of the Green Party in the previous Dáil, was moved into the position of Ceann Comharile. The other main casualty was outgoing Minister for the Environment Dick Roche.

The entrance protocol also highlighted the extent to which Fianna Fáil wanted to reinforce the idea of the continuance of 'government as usual'. The underlying message was that the government was largely unchanged, with the

Greens being a mere add-on. That said, the two ministries gained – Environment, Heritage and Local Government and Communication, Energy and Natural Resources – were significant, with the capacity to influence change in many areas.

Some changes that the Greens didn't want to see were happening even before the government was formed. In his last days of office, Dick Roche signed a ministerial order allowing the covering of an important megalithic burial chamber at Lismullen to permit construction of the agreed route for the M3 motorway. This motorway, and its proximity to national monuments in and around Tara, was an important item of discussion during the programme for government negotiations. Noel Dempsey had told us that the decision on Lismullen would be made by the Minister for the Environment. We took this to mean that the decision would be on the desk for John Gormley as and when he took office. In our naivety, we did not seek a written commitment to this. On our first day in government, we were being undermined.

A second surprise was the announcement of the Ministers for State. Trevor received a position at the Department of Agriculture as Minister for Food and Agriculture, an ideal position for him, and one in which he would invest an enormous amount of energy. Some allowance for Green sensitivities seemed to have been made when Frank Fahey was not reappointed. He had been strongly criticised in the previous Dáil by Trevor Sargent, and we would have not taken his reappointment lightly.

What we did take lightly was Bertie Ahern's decision to appoint 20 Ministers for State. We were stunned at such a naked exercise of political jobbery. It was done cynically, knowing that in our first week of office there was very little *that* we could do about it. It was never discussed with us. We made efforts later in the life of the government to reverse the decision.

We were aware that the Fianna Fáil strategy was to put the Greens in a box and keep us there. The spinning of the political journalists was about how Fianna Fáil had master-fully bested us in negotiations and about how they would treat us as their 'partners' in government. One particular example around this time was an article written by Sam Smyth for the *Irish Independent*. In it he claimed, based on good Fianna Fáil sources, that the negotiations had begun with Brian Cowen thumping the table saying that, with regards to changes to live animal transport, that Fianna Fáil wouldn't have any of that. It never happened. In fact, I can't even remember the topic being discussed. We would have known that it was a matter for European Union directives, and that any changes could only be made there. That didn't seem to matter, as it was the mythology that was impor-tant to Fianna Fáil and unimportant to us. In retrospect, this would become a cardinal error for us. Leaving half-formed impressions to take hold damaged how we wanted to be perceived.

The Fianna Fáil ministers did at least want to put an appearance of a Green veneer on the new government. The Cabinet travelled in a minibus to Áras an Uachtaráin to receive their seals of office and hold their first Cabinet meeting. None were to emulate John Gormley and Eamon Ryan by cycling to their department offices.

In the first weeks of the new government there was a rush to put our team in place. In both government depart-ments it was done relatively quickly. In the Department of the Environment, Heritage and Local Government, John took parliamentary researcher Ryan Meade to become his political advisor. Ryan had been an able lieutenant of John's for several years. He briefly served as a member of Dublin City Council, replacing Eamon Ryan in a seat that had originally been won by John. With his policy advisor, John caused some surprise – he selected David Healy. David had been elected in his early twenties as part of the first crop of Green Party councillors in 1991. He was initially a member of Dublin County Council, then subsequently Fingal County Council. In those early days he was thought to be part of the party's awkward squad, questioning anything and everything. Despite that, he was a very proficient public representative and few in the party could match his knowledge on policy, particularly environmental policy. It was a clever appointment by John.

In appointing a press officer for his department, John also thought outside the box. Even in opposition, the Greens had never received a particularly fair press, but for press officers we weren't looking for ideologues, but fair-minded people who were able to present what we were about in the fairest possible way. John had admired the work of Liam Reid writing for *The Irish Times*. It seemed an ideal fit. A similar process was carried out for the position of Deputy Government Press spokesperson. Harry Magee, then with *The Irish Times*, was approached. He strongly considered coming over to the other side before eventually deciding that his future lay in political journalism. He declined the position, suggesting that John Downing be approached.

John had had a distinguished career in journalism, starting with a local newspaper in Limerick, continuing on to the *Kerryman* and the *Irish Examiner* before becoming the political editor of the *Irish Daily Star*. From this last position he was about to take a break to go back to education. Becoming a government spokesperson is something he wouldn't have thought about, nor was he likely to be considered for it. He was chosen, and with his laconic style he brought something very interesting to the mix.

Eamon Ryan's staff came with a lot less complication. Claire Byrne and Sue Duke, who had worked with Eamon as a TD, followed him into the department. Claire ran his constituency office while Sue was taken on as a political advisor. For press officer Eamon head-hunted Bríd McGrath, who had impressed him when he had come across her while she was working for the Department of Foreign Affairs.

The key appointment took the longest to fill. The position of Programme Manager working in the Department of the Taoiseach was to be the eyes and ears of the Green Party in regards to the rest of the government. Many names were thought of, but an initial approach was made to someone whom I had suggested, Cork solicitor Joe Noonan. Joe had tremendous campaigning experience, which when added to his legal expertise would have been a considerable benefit to us in government. Joe was given several days to consider whether he wanted to accept the job. As part of a successful legal practice, accepting would have meant a drop in income for an uncertain period of time, not knowing how long the government would stay in place. His biggest reservation would have been the impending European Union treaty referendum. As an inveterate campaigner against previous EU treaties, I suspect this would have been a major factor in his decision not to accept to post.

At this stage, John Gormley asked whether I would be prepared to accept the position. I wouldn't, and wasn't prepared to even consider it. At twice the salary and likely half the hassle maybe I should have, but I wanted to continue in a front of house position on behalf of the party. Fortunately, we already had a likely candidate for programme manager. Party General Secretary Donal Geoghegan had already had considerable experience of social partnership, and the many workings of government and the civil service. He wasn't originally suggested as there were concerns about how it might affect the party's own infrastructure. Despite that, he was needed for the new position, which set in motion of series of musical chairs in the party as we adjusted to the business of being in government.

Aoife Ní Lochlainn joined Donal Geoghegan in the Programme for Government office. They were to become a formidable team. Donal was replaced as General Secretary by Colm O'Caomhánaigh, who was the parliamentary group secretary. Colm in turn was replaced by Niall O'Brolcháin.

***

Not only jobs within government needed to be filled. A subsequent rejigging of the paid posts in the Green Party and the resignation of Trevor Sargent as Party Leader meant that party members had a very important decision now to make.

Voting was by postal ballot. Two nominations were received: those of John Gormley and former member of the European Parliament Patricia McKenna. The party was being offered a good choice. In so far as 'realo' and 'fundi' factions existed within the Irish Green Party, they were represented by John and Patricia. They also respectively personified those sections of the party that wanted to be in, or out, of government. It wasn't widely known that, despite these divergent positions, as long-time party members John and Patricia greatly respected each other and were very good friends.

There would be no certainty of success for John in this election. As part of the alternative, non-conformist tradition of the Greens, many felt that the position of leader should be held by a person who was not part of the Cabinet, and that it would it be another useful counterpoint if the position were held by someone who was not supportive of the decision to enter government.

When the result was announced, John had won by a two-to-one margin, which gave a relatively strong mandate. The party now had its second elected leader, one with a very different style from Trevor Sargent.

John's election created a vacancy for Party Chair. In the parliamentary party I had already let others know of my interest in challenging for this position. By this stage, the Dáil summer recess had begun. This provided valuable space to allow for staff to be appointed, Ministers to read into their brief, and for the party in general to be reorganised. It was decided that the election for Party Chair should involve a campaign of several months to go around the country and meet the party members in an effort to discover where the soul of the party lay.

In the meantime, the Seanad Elections had to be organised. Several Green councillors had already expressed their unhappiness at having to vote for Fianna Fáil candidates. A factor for some was whether they would be considered for the two Green Seanad positions agreed as a condition of entering government.

It was agreed that the councillors should have a ballot, a non-binding ballot amongst themselves, to indicate who they thought should be proposed to John Gormley to be the party's Seanad representatives. Everyone was to be part of this process. I wasn't happy that so many assumed that I was to be given a Seanad seat. This assumption existed beyond the Green Party. In Leinster House I regularly met Brian Cowen, invariably in the Members' Bar, where he would make comments along the lines of 'Shouldn't you be out with your electorate?' It's hard to know if he was being snide or humorous, but I didn't like it.

The Green councillors agreed that they should propose to John Gormley that I be nominated for the first Seanad seat. A vote took place on the second nominated position. I felt that, both on grounds of best electoral performance and for gender balance reasons, Déirdre de Búrca represented the best choice. Deirdre would not have been the best networker within the Green councillor group. To secure a nomination was likely to be very difficult for Deirdre. Mark Dearey had a strong case on electoral performance grounds. Niall O'Brolcháin with his Galway base made a case on geographical grounds. High profile councillors Bronwen Maher and Tony McDermott also had strong cases to make.

While electoral performance remained the most important priority in selecting candidates for Seanad, we still considered questions of gender and geography to be relevant. The Seanad positions allowed the party to increase the number of women in our parliamentary party – something that had long been of concern to us. Our sensitivity to geographical factors grew from the awareness that the parliamentary party remained dominated by Dublin-based representatives.

The electorate consisted of all the elected Green public representatives. Thus, it included the parliamentary party but did not include me. The final ballot had seven candidates, which included Patricia McKenna, who interestingly finished in seventh place once the votes had been counted.

Against the odds, mainly because of strong support from the parliamentary party, Déirdre de Búrca won the vote. While John Gormley had said that he would directly act on the recommendations of the councillor group, he had the power to recommend whomever he wanted. He had difficulty recommending Deirdre, whom he felt would not use the Seanad position to build upon the recent general election result. It took an awful lot of lobbying by Eamon Ryan and I to persuade John otherwise.

The internal contest decided, attention turned to the Seanad elections themselves. Green councillors were still put out at being told for which Fianna Fáil candidates to vote. My role was to convince them to do so, and to see to it that as much party discipline could be maintained as possible. The Green votes did largely hold. Those councillors who wouldn't vote for a proscribed list ended up voting for their own preferred Fianna Fáil candidates. This saw Fianna Fáil win two more Seanad seats than they had expected.

It was several more weeks before the Taoiseach nominees were announced. In early August I was taking a long-promised holiday with my wife Bláithín in St Petersburg, specially to visit the Hermitage gallery. It was promised regardless of what happened in the election, and meant as some compensation for what being in politics had done to our lives.

While there I received a call from the Taoiseach's office. 'Would you take a call from the Taoiseach later?' I was asked. There never was a further phone call. I was never asked if I wanted to be a member of the Seanad. Neither was Déirdre de Búrca.

That Sunday, while still in St Petersburg, I agreed to talk about the new Seanad on the RTÉ 1 morning radio show being presented by Rachel English. I was doing the interview on my mobile phone, and was finding it difficult to find a quiet enough place in which I could take the call. In the end, I did the interview from the toilet of a Pizza Hut off Nevsky Prospect!

The Taoiseach's Seanad selection was certainly curious. Six of the eleven were Fianna Fáil people chosen for electoral considerations. Two Greens were chosen, as were two Progressive Democrats in the form of Fiona O'Malley and Ciaran Cannon. That what was left of the Progressive Democrats secured two Seanad seats certainly let us know our place in the pecking order. The eleventh nominee was the surprising and somewhat colourful choice, Eoghan Harris, and his nomination was seen as rewarding his performance on *The Late Late Show* during the general election campaign.

We hadn't sought the position of Tánaiste in the Dáil, but we did seek the position of Deputy Leader of Seanad Éireann. It is the lowest ranked of all government appointments. Not being a constitutional position, it paid a stipend of €7,000 a year. We felt that it was important as a signal of our being a separate political party and of our having a distinct role to play in the life of the Seanad.

The fact that I was to be made Deputy Leader of the Seanad seemed to come as something of a surprise to the actual Leader of the Seanad, Donie Cassidy, when I met him in the car park of Leinster House a number of days before the first sitting of the 23rd Seanad. It wasn't to be our first experience of seeing how poor the internal communications in Fianna Fáil could be.

The issue of Seanad reform was an issue that very important to the Greens. In our first private members time we highlighted the issue. John Gormley established an all-party committee to pursue the issue. Independent Senator Joe O'Toole rightly pointed out at the time that we would get zero cooperation from Fianna Fáil on this.

We had our own internal business to arrange. The hustings for our Party Chair/Cathaoirleach were taking place. I had first announced my intention to run to the parliamentary party, hoping to get their collective support, however Paul Gogarty subsequently announced that he too would like to make his case for the position. Our Dublin City

Councillor Bronwen Maher would also be a strong candidate. Party activists John Barry and Phil Kearney completed the line-up.

The hustings were conducted in an extremely polite atmosphere. The party activists seemed to be in good heart. Members were certainly being given a choice between different visions of the party, and more specifically concerning what the role of Party Chair should be. For me, with the party in government, the Party Chair had to be the person expressing the distinctiveness and independence of the party, in ways that those in the Cabinet, restricted by confidentiality and collective responsibility, could not.

The election was held under a 'preferendum' voting system developed by longstanding party member Peter Emerson. Under this system, voting choices are weighted. This election was the first significant use of this system, and it caused some bemusement, especially among the media. Thankfully, my pitch to the party members was accepted. It was where I wanted to be; it was what I wanted to be doing.

The political agenda was focused on preparation for the Estimates and Budget 2008. The economic climate was showing some causes for concern. Projected growth rates were not being met. Tax projections would be two billion euro down on what was hoped for in Budget 2007.

Despite this, independent agencies such as the Economic and Social Research Institute (ESRI) and the Central Bank were saying that GNP growth in 2008 was likely to be 3.25%, with projected GDP growth anticipated at 3.5%. In its commentary, the ESRI was warning that the slowdown in construction would have a negative effect on growth, with an expected 1.2% decrease in growth with each 10,000 fewer housing units built! My own role, even as the Green Party's Finance Spokesperson, in influencing Budget 2008 was very limited. As Minister for Finance, Brian Cowen limited decisions on the budget strictly to the Cabinet.

Despite a general lack of access and influence, several measures were included that had an identifiable Green print. John Gormley was successful in arguing for a change of the system of vehicle registration tax from engine size to an emissions-based system. Eamon successfully brought about a new tax relief to encourage the purchase and development of energy-saving equipment.

I worked with our programme for government people in meeting with Department of Finance officials and talking through the submissions that we had made. It was clear to me that Brian Cowen had decided to limit – and where possible, avoid – Green Party input into this budget. Not being able to directly influence budgetary policy at this stage was a major mistake on our part. While it was our first experience of this process, which could be put down to naivety, to have adopted a more strident approach then would have avoided the scale of some of the decisions that subsequently had to be made.

Budget 2008 took too much of a 'business as usual' approach to the public finances, continuing the dangerous trends of previous budgets of increasing public expenditure combined with tax changes that would soon spiral out of control. There continued to be no real questioning of this process. Opposition parties were demanding greater levels of public expenditure again. Media interests, especially the Independent Group of newspapers, were whipping something close to a hysteria with their flawed belief that high property prices could best be tackled by reducing Stamp Duty.

This was the time to put on the brakes. While the levels of increase in public spending, particularly social welfare rates and public sector pay, were rising at a lower level and at a slower speed than before, the fact that spending was rising at all was the wrong approach to take, even then.

Of course, secrecy is vitally important in any budgetary process. Knowing this, we were surprised that the proposal to radically change Stamp Duty was only made known at a Cabinet meeting a couple of hours before the Minister for Finance made his Budget speech. Had there been a prior discussion of this measure, we would have questioned why such a change was being put in place. The last thing we felt was needed was yet another measure designed to pump-prime an already inflated property market. We would have preferred measures to help dampen a rapidly spiralling construction sector.

One measure on which we had insisted as a programme for government commitment was the introduction of a parallel Carbon Budget to be presented by the Minister for the Environment on the day after the Minister for Finance's budget speech. This became counterproductive. I suspect that it fed into a belief within Fianna Fáil, expressed through Brian Cowen, that the Greens should not be fully involved in the formulation of the government's economic policy. This would best be achieved, it was thought, by keeping the Greens in their box.

It was clear that Fianna Fáil was indifferent to idea of a Carbon Budget, but so were the opposition parties, and, it must be said, the general media. John Gormley wasn't looking forward to his first Carbon Budget either. He didn't feel that he had enough to say. In truth, he hadn't, because for a carbon budget to be effective it would need to be explained in financial terms. Central to the financial basis of a carbon budget would be the existence of a Carbon Levy/Tax, which Brian Cowen and Fianna Fáil had successfully kicked into touch for the medium term into the consideration of the Commission on Taxation.

The changes in motor tax had already been announced in the previous day's budget. John could and would refer to it, but he was anxious that the Carbon Budget would be too slight. His big idea was to speed up the process of transfer from traditional light-bulbs to CFL energy-saving lighting. The European Union was already committed to achieving this change within a number of years, but John felt that Ireland could be ahead of this curve and lead change in Europe, as had been achieved with the plastic bag levy. It seemed like a good idea. It was being promoted with the best of motivations, but it would soon form part of the cartoon image that would surround the Greens in government.

As the Dáil rose in mid-December for the Christmas recess, we had already served six months in government. All the necessary adjustments had been made. The learning period had passed. From there on in, there could be no more excuses.

5 | The Long Goodbye

The period in Irish politics that follows the Christmas recess is usually relatively uncontentious. The public reaction to the Budget has usually subsided, with most political junkies awaiting the provisions of Finance Bill to see if any more surprises await the taxpayers. 2007 promised to follow that pattern.

The end of the year opinion polls were showing quite well for the government. The Green Party figure was up on that achieved during the general election. John Gormley was being listed as the second most popular political leader behind Bertie Ahern. It was still the honeymoon period, but there seemed to be no adverse reaction from Green Party supporters to the decision to enter into government with Fianna Fáil.

The additional provisions of the Finance Bill provided no real surprises. One provision that I had included as a Green Party initiative was a benefit-in-kind charge to those availing of free parking in city centre districts. As this was a provision that would largely affect civil and public servants, there already had been a difficulty in proposing this and having it added to the bill. Implementing the measure would subsequently prove impossible. Another lesson learned in challenging vested interests in Irish society.

Within the Green Party, we had some housekeeping to do. Later in the year a referendum would be held on the Treaty of Lisbon, amending the European treaties. This would be difficult. While it wasn't part of the programme for government agreement, it was assumed that the government would have a common position recommending approval of the Treaty.

The Green Party had opposed all previous European treaties. Opposition was never of the kneejerk variety. Our concerns over the democratic deficit in the European Union, ambiguities over military alliances and the economic direction of Europe were subsequently in many respects justified. Our opposition to the Treaty of Maastricht, based on concerns regarding the weaknesses in the proposed moves towards a European currency, would prove to be all too real.

Communicating our approach to Europe was always difficult for the Irish Greens. Differences of approach also existed with other European Green parties. Where we did agree was that we wanted to help bring about a better European Union. The Nice Treaty had created something of an administrative mess, and while the Treaty of Lisbon was far from ideal, it did at least seek to repair some of the worst aspects of the Nice Treaty.

To have a party position meant undergoing a full debate among our members. Spearheading the case for supporting the treaty was Déirdre de Búrca. Déirdre had been associated with a strong negative position towards the European Union in previous referendum campaigns. As the party's European spokesperson, she had steered the party towards a more nuanced position.

In January 2008, a special party convention was organised, held in the Hilton Hotel next to the Grand Canal in Dublin. The party's constitution required that any policy position required a two thirds majority of those present. The key intervention was that of Joe Noonan, who had been a 'People First' European Election candidate in 1989. His contribution sowed enough doubt in members' minds. The final result saw 63% vote in favour of the motion. Another half a dozen votes and the motion would have passed.

It wasn't necessarily the worst of results. While officially the party couldn't support the treaty, it did show that a significant number of our members supported the process. It also freed John Gormley and Eamon Ryan to be able to speak in favour of the government's position.

As it happened, events at the Mahon Tribunal were making happenings at Leinster House, and at Government Buildings, increasingly irrelevant in any case. The Tribunal recommenced public hearings after the general election in September 2007. It was claiming, rather optimistically, that its work would be completed within another year. Hearings were being recommenced with a module that concentrated largely on the personal finances of Taoiseach. A string of high-profile witnesses were to be heard, distracting hugely from the business of government.

In the Greens, we had made a strategic decision that we would not react to every piece of evidence that came before the tribunal. We would not be, we said, the moral guardians of Fianna Fáil. Our preference was to wait for the findings of the tribunal, expecting those criticised by such findings to act accordingly. Our thinking was informed by the fact that we felt that the Progressive Democrats had not responded well or correctly when dealing with tribunals in the past. We were determined to act differently, and not to be seen to be the lighted touch-paper whenever anything of even the mildest controversy was being said at the tribunal.

We adopted this studied distance from the happenings at the tribunal to the extent that we never asked, prior to the giving of any evidence by members of the government, whether there would be issues of concern that would be raised. Nor did we raise the question during negotiations on becoming part of government. The tribunal existed, and as far as we were concerned that was the mechanism for providing answers that would be provided in due course.

Press leaks in December presaged that the forthcoming module at the Mahon Tribunal would be concentrating on Bertie Ahern and his finances. This increased the political temperature, with the opposition promising to raise the issue when the Dáil reconvened. There also seemed to be a co-ordinated attempt within Fianna Fáil to denigrate the tribunal and its workings.

The Dáil reconvened on January 30th. One of the first items of business was a Fine Gael private members motion asking the House to reaffirm its confidence in the Mahon Tribunal. Given the stirrings of agitation that had been sprinkled about by various Fianna Fáil ministers over the previous weeks, it was clear to the Greens that this was a motion that Fianna Fáil wanted to take on, or at the very least show ambivalence towards.

The idea of being indifferent towards the Mahon Tribunal appalled us. The original draft of the government countermotion contained no statement of confidence in its workings. As the Minister under whose department's auspices the Mahon Tribunal came, John Gormley refused to move a countermotion until such a statement was included. This was to be the new wording that John Gormley would move:

To delete all words after "Dáil Éireann" and substitute the following:

"... affirms its confidence in the Mahon Tribunal and believes it will fulfil the tribunal's mandate pursuant

to the amended terms of reference established by the Oireachtas;

notes that the tribunal was established to inquire urgently into certain planning matters and report to the Clerk of the Dáil and make such findings and recommendations as it sees fit;

notes the rulings of the Supreme Court in relation to the tribunal of inquiry's terms of reference;

notes the projected cost of this tribunal of inquiry, urges the tribunal to continue its work and looks forward to receiving the report of the tribunal expeditiously, in order that the Dáil may debate and deliberate on its findings;

urges the early consideration and enactment by the Oireachtas of the Tribunals of Inquiry Bill 2005 to underpin the confidence of the public and the Oireachtas in any future tribunals and to address matters of procedure and practice in the conduct of any such tribunals;

welcomes the opportunity to discuss the procedures and practices involved in investigating matters mandated by Oireachtas Éireann; and

condemns the leaking of tribunal documents as a breach of confidentiality as established by law, and an infringement on the rights of those affected, and supports appropriate actions to investigate such leaks, and further reaffirms the right to confidentiality to which each citizen is entitled in their correspondence with the tribunal."

Bertie Ahern himself was to be one of the first witnesses to this module of the tribunal. He used the opportunity to reject the allegations made by the builder Tom Gilmartin that he taken large sums of money from the developer

Owen O'Callaghan. Nothing seemed to be added to this mix by his appearance. He had something of an advantage in 'getting his retaliation in first' before Tom Gilmartin would make his appearance in front of the tribunal.

Gilmartin was the next witness, and he gave lengthy and detailed evidence to the tribunal. Much of his evidence had been leaked in advance, so again it seemed that little had been added. Government Minister Micheál Martin made an appearance before the tribunal before Christmas 2007. He also was in denial mode, and the denials made it difficult to add to the ongoing controversy. I did do a personal double take, though, when he admitted that he had accepted a 5,000 Punt donation from Owen O'Callaghan for the 1991 local elections. That single donation was a multiple of what I spent on being elected to Cork Corporation that year.

The start of 2008 saw the same pattern being repeated at the tribunal. A complication soon arose, however, when Bertie Ahern decided to take a High Court action against the tribunal. We weren't delighted that a head of government was taking a constitutional action against a tribunal that had been established by the Oireachtas. We rationalised the action by our belief that it was a personal action by and on behalf of Bertie Ahern; it was not a government decision. It required no prior consultation or ongoing involvement on our part. Nevertheless, the taking of the action made us extremely uncomfortable. An eventual decision by the High Court would be an obvious future pressure point for the government.

I said as much in a radio programme at the time on the Newstalk station with Eamon Keane. Eamon was and is a friend, but no quarter was ever given by him whenever I took part on his programme. I expressed my unhappiness at the Taoiseach's taking of this legal action. I went on to say that I believed that it reflected concern that existed in the party. Eamon encouraged me to say some other things that I probably didn't want to say. I didn't think that I had said anything new or surprising, but it became a minor news story because of the context in which it was said.

Asked about Ahern's immediate future as Taoiseach, I said that as a party we had entered government with the expectation, due to statements that he had already made, that before the end of the lifetime of the government Bertie Ahern would have stood down. That was no secret. What was taken as new was my assertion that as a party we expected to be told in advance of when that was likely to happen.

It was an interview that obviously did not go down too well with many in Fianna Fáil, although not all seemed to be unhappy with the message that was being sent out. While not too publicly apparent, behind the scenes some movement against Ahern was fermenting in Fianna Fáil.

A Green colleague of mine, working with Trevor Sargent in the Department of Agriculture, told me of a snippet he overheard when walking down the ministerial corridor at that time. When passing the office of the Minister for Agriculture, he heard, with characteristic volume and lack of restraint, the Minister utter: 'I see that fucker Boyle has grown a pair of balls.'

The Taoiseach was given leave in February 2008 to move his action. The chorus of claim, counterclaim and denial had meant that the tribunal was waning in terms of public consciousness and interest. However, a witness was soon to appear who would change the public's perception of Bertie Ahern for the worse.

***

On March 20th Gráinne Carruth, Ahern's former secretary, was called to give evidence to the tribunal. In what was an emotional and trying testimony, Ms Carruth broke down when confronted with evidence that her prior contention that all monies she had lodged on his behalf related only to his salary cheques can't have been true, as some of the lodgements were made in foreign currencies. The testimony was damaging enough, but the distancing that followed by Bertie Ahern, of someone who must have been a long time loyal employee, seemed to instantly dissolve the Teflon-like veneer that had surround him throughout his political career.

Aside from the probity issues involved, we in the Greens were as appalled with the brutal coldness of his behaviour as many members of the public were. We couldn't see, though, any way in which we could directly intervene whilst remaining consistent with our policy that we would not interfere with or be seen to react to the happenings at the tribunal. Events overtook us in any case.

After a number of days of public disquiet, a number of heads started to appear over the parapet. First to give her opinion in another interview on Newstalk was my Seanad colleague, and like myself a Taoiseach's nominee, Fiona O'Malley, still a Progressive Democrat senator. She called on Bertie Ahern to make a clarifying statement.

Ordinarily this might have been brushed aside, but when she was supported by her Progressive Democrat colleague, the Minister for Health and Children Mary Harney, alarm bells began to sound for Ahern. The Mary Harney statement in particular forced John Gormley to similarly call for a statement. It was talked about by the Green parliamentary party, but questions of content and timing were left to John Gormley. Now there seemed an inevitability about Bertie Ahern's term as Taoiseach coming to a close.

Mary Harney and John Gormley made their statements on March 27th. On the following Sunday, on *The Week In Politics* programme on RTÉ, the Minister for Agriculture and Food Mary Coughlan added to the temperature by refusing to answer a question several times on whether the Taoiseach had her full support. In refusing to do so she was seen as a stalking-horse for Brian Cowen, now seen to be making his move behind the scenes in Fianna Fáil.

All this activity was occurring while the Dáil wasn't sitting, it being on a two-week Easter break. The Dáil was due to reconvene on Wednesday April 2nd. From the start of that week, speculation became feverish. On Tuesday evening, events were happening of which few were aware. Brian Cowen met Bertie Ahern, where he informed him of his intention to resign as Taoiseach. John Gormley was told on that evening too, but asked not to tell anyone else, which he didn't. The rest of us received texts from John Downing, Deputy Government Press Secretary, in the morning, telling us to look out for an announcement by the Taoiseach being made early that morning from the steps of Government Buildings.

The announcement, when it was made, still came as a surprise. He hadn't been pushed; at least not by us. Further surprises came as the content of the announcement was in typical Ahern terms: less than straightforward. The announcement was not a resignation with immediate effect, but an intention to resign that would be given effect over a month later on May 6th.

It was understood that a changeover would take at least a couple of weeks, to allow for a Fianna Fáil leadership election. Over a month seemed a bit too much. Still, as much of an additional distraction as it was to the business of government, we didn't say anything and waited for the process to work itself out. From a Green point of view, the contents of the announcement presented less of a problem than the likely public and media perception of the government. A brief Cabinet meeting, in which Bertie Ahern informed the entire Cabinet of his intention to resign, preceded the Government Buildings announcement. Cabinet members were invited to accompany the Taoiseach when facing the media. Not all ministers made that journey. Prominent amongst those surrounding the Taoiseach were Brian Cowen, Brian Lenihan and Mary Harney (a Progressive Democrat, but very much an embedded part of the Government for the previous 11 years). Eamon Ryan chose not to take part, leaving John Gormley with something of a dilemma. As leader of the minority party in government, he made the decision that he would be present, because his absence would have been remarked upon. In retrospect, it was something he would come to regret.

I suspect that Ahern didn't enjoy his last 11 months in office. The long goodbye seemed to be dictated by commitments that had already been entered into, as well as a need to solidify Ahern's legacy. In February 2008, Ahern had received an invitation to address the joint Houses of Congress in Washington on April 30th. Another major event that had been pencilled into his diary was a dedication ceremony at the Battle of the Boyne site with Ian Paisley, who, in an act of neat political symmetry, had also announced his intention to resign as First Minister in the Northern Ireland Executive.

I attended the event at the Boyne. There is no doubt that the occasion was marked with a certain poignancy. Both men deserved to have their individual and joint contributions to the changed political atmosphere on the island honoured.

Bertie Ahern's wider legacy would not be sustained by such an event. His economic policies were reckless. The boom, at least from 2002 onwards, was superficial and was allowed to grow out of control. Ireland became more unequal. There were signs that he himself was becoming increasingly aware of this. His infamous July 2007 speech, made just three weeks after the Greens had entered government, stating that those who were talking down the economy could go and commit suicide, indicated an awareness that his legacy was starting to go awry.

Outside of a number of measures in the first few weeks of government – the increase in the number of junior ministers, increases in ministerial pay, and a piece of legislation that seemed to exist for no reason other than to improve the pension entitlements of former minister Michael Woods – he seemed to be fair to the Greens and our participation in government. 'Fair' as in 'businesslike', in the sense of adhering to the agreements we had reached. Did we have our reservations? Of course, but we had committed to having these resolved through the tribunal process. All deserve to be considered innocent until proven guilty. Without proof, suspicions counted for nothing, which is why the tribunal was so important.

Ahern's resignation would be seen as the first opportunity under which the Greens could and should have left government. To have left after just 10 months, though, would have confirmed the criticisms of many who claimed that the Greens lacked the backbone to be in government under these difficult circumstances. To have left then would have carried no guarantee of bringing down the government in any event. For the Greens, leaving at that point would have put the future of the tribunal at risk, and it would have meant leaving government without passing a Planning Bill, which was a centrepiece of our legislation programme. This bill was to be our response to the corruption that caused the Mahon Tribunal, and was a prime reason for remaining in government.

***

The real attention was being given to the question of who would succeed Bertie Ahern as leader of Fianna Fáil and Taoiseach. Brian Cowen was the obvious front runner, expected to win even in the event of a challenge. There were likely to be other contenders – Brian Lenihan, Micheál Martin, Dermot Ahern, Noel Dempsey and Mary Hanafin. None came to the fore, probably realising that continued Cabinet membership was better than the making of a challenge that in all likelihood would not succeed.

Bertie Ahern made his announcement on April 2nd. Brian Cowen announced his intention to stand on April 4th, having been proposed by Brian Lenihan (eliminating him from any contest) and seconded by Mary Coughlan. By April 9th, nominations for leader of Fianna Fáil had closed, and none of the other likely candidates had put their names forward. Brian Cowen was thus elected unopposed. In another four weeks, he would be Taoiseach.

At this time, the *Sunday Business Post* commissioned a Red C poll to measure voting intentions and gauge the public's view on Brian Cowen becoming Taoiseach. The vast majority of the respondents felt that he would be a good Taoiseach and that he would represent a safe pair of hands. However, a majority also felt that he wasn't charismatic, nor was he someone who could be warmed to.

The political party figures in that poll were also interesting. Fianna Fáil at 40% was maintaining the level of support it had achieved in the previous year's general election. At 28% and 11% respectively, Fine Gael and the Labour Party were also little changed. Sinn Féin was posting a 6% figure. After almost a year in government, the Green Party was now registering at a historic high of 9%, almost twice the support level won in the general election.

Bertie Ahern's resignation as Taoiseach neatly coincided with the Green Party's annual convention, which was being held in Dundalk. Louth was a target area for the party, and we were anxious to promote Dundalk Town Councillor Mark Dearey as a future Oireachtas member for the area. After 10 months in office it was a good opportunity to take stock. The Taoiseach's resignation also meant that an air of uncertainty about future participation was starting to develop.

On the surface, the convention was again well organised by Karen Devine and her team, designed to fit in with the requirements of television broadcast. There were some uniquely Green elements to the fringe of the convention. The relative closeness of Dundalk to Dublin saw a bicycle ride organised by Cork member Johnny O'Mahony. Those who took part included Tony McDermott, a South Dublin County Councillor and Niamh FitzGibbon from Wexford. They were seen off by John Gormley from his office at the Customs House. En route they were joined by Trevor Sargent and Stiofáin Nutty in Balbriggan before heading for Dundalk.

A real problem for the organisers of the convention was how to achieve coverage for the party when the media agenda was dominated by the resignation of a Taoiseach and the succession race within Fianna Fáil. Coverage did come, and it was surprising. John Gormley's first speech as party leader contained a section committing the party in government to seek to improve international human rights. A reference to Tibet offended the Chinese ambassador, who publicly walked out during the live television broadcast.

It hadn't been contrived. John had long had a personal interest in Tibet. When he was Lord Mayor of Dublin in 1994/95, he had wanted to give the Freedom of the City to the Dalai Lama, but failed to receive support from other political parties. Nevertheless, the incident brought attention to the convention or the party.

Another political sideshow was the slow, lingering death of the Progressive Democrats. It was something we had anticipated, but it hardly added to government stability. Around this time, Mary Harney relinquished her caretaker leadership of that party and was replaced by Senator Ciarán Cannon who, like me, had been a Taoiseach's nominee to the Seanad.

Meanwhile, back in the real world, Brian Cowen's elevation to the position of Taoiseach was accompanied by a triumphal tour of his Dáil constituency in Laois/Offaly. The images of speaking from truck platforms and singing songs seemed to hark back to another time. There would definitely be a cultural change with this change of leadership, that much was clear. Less clear was whether this change would be for the better.

As a party, we had mixed feelings about Brian Cowen taking over as a Taoiseach. We didn't doubt his ability, but from the outset he had hardly seemed warm to the idea of being in government with the Greens. His ascension, though it may be hard to believe in the light of subsequent events, was being well received by the public and the media. There was a fear that he may have called an early general election to cash in on this perceived popularity.

On the other hand, the change of office could be good, we thought. It was an opportunity to change direction and recast the government. In this regard, his choice of Cabinet did not inspire. Too many of the people promoted seemed to know Brian Cowen well rather than possessing any previous acknowledged ability. One choice was interesting: that of Brian Lenihan to be the next Minister for Finance. He had been overlooked for too long by Bertie Ahern. As Minister for Justice we had been happy to see that he was close to our way of thinking on many of those issues. However, he had never had any previous experience of an economic ministry. He had to read himself into the job, but had the intellectual capacity to achieve that. The inverse of that was that his replacement as Minister for Justice, Dermot Ahern, was not someone we were confident was disposed to a Green viewpoint on justice issues.

At that point, we feared an early election because, despite a year in government, we were being frustrated and stymied on many policy areas. One example was the approaching referendum on the Lisbon Treaty. For several months, our party spokesperson on the issue Déirdre de Búrca had participated in a series of meetings with the Minister for Foreign Affairs (now Micheál Martin), and with officials from his department and the Department of Defence, to agree on a wording for the referendum that showed that Ireland was at least being more proactive in acknowledging the policy of neutrality. Issues that were meant to be followed up on after each meeting rarely were, and at each new meeting she was met with civil servants armed with a new set of excuses on why progress hadn't happened and why it might not occur.

Ciarán Cuffe was having an even worse experience in a series of meetings with the new Minister for Justice, Dermot Ahern, over how to bring legislation on allowing Gardaí to board planes at Shannon to ensure that 'extraordinary renditions' were not occurring. Little or no progress was being seen. Taunting, from the Labour Party in particular, was making this a touchstone issue for us. The constant repetition of the chant 'Tara, Shannon, Rossport' exaggerated both the priority that we applied to each of these issues and our ability to effect change in them. Nevertheless, it had the effect of undermining the confidence of Green supporters.

The change in the Department of Justice also slowed down progress on the Civil Partnership Bill, in which we had invested a considerable amount of political capital. Along with Ciarán Cuffe, interaction with Dermot Ahern and his officials was by being led on behalf of the Greens by Roderic O'Gorman. O'Gorman and the rest of the party were considerably frustrated by the foot-dragging approach adopted by the Minister and his department, a sign of a socially conservative fear of the change being proposed.

On Tara, we were wrong-footed before our first day of government. John Gormley acted quickly to appoint a long-time critic of the M3 motorway route, Professor Conor Newman of NUI Galway, as chair of a special committee to oversee archaeological work on the route. Later he was also appointed as chair of the Heritage Council. Gormley, through ministerial order, restricted future building development along the route, thereby limiting any increase in the value of the land that may have been anticipated by some.

On Shannon, we were subjected to interminable prevarication. The establishing of a Cabinet sub-committee in September 2008 gave us hope that legislation would be forthcoming. It never came. Future WikiLeaks revelations alleging US concerns regarding the changes we sought, and acknowledging that some of the planes that had landed there were used in rendition, were never communicated to the Greens.

We had failed to get legislation of the question of rendition, but on one occasion pressure from the Green Party did result in a place being boarded at Shannon. John Gormley, having been contacted by campaigners monitoring the airport, did succeed in having one plane boarded. It contained a golf party.

The lack of progress on rendition did allow some moral capital to be built up that allowed Ireland, because of Green Party pushing, to be one of the first countries (and few countries) to accept people who had been illegally detained at Guantanamo Bay.

At least on Rossport, and the issue of the Corrib Gas field, we had the ability to proceed at our own pace. We didn't speed up the process, but we ensured that ultimate decisions had to be made using a renewed process of public consultation. Despite this, our critics did not acknowledge any efforts we were making. That the critics had such differing levels of criticism made finding a possible solution very difficult. For some, it was the question of an onshore or an offshore terminal. The main issue centred around the route of the gas pipeline, with the attendant health and safety concerns that were being voiced. With these concerns, tensions were to rise between Eamon Ryan and John Gormley. The proposed pipeline route went through a Special Area of Conservation, which was a cause for concern to the Minister for the Environment.

Other Rossport critics were exercised with the deal that had been agreed by the then Energy Minister, Ray Burke, which was claimed to hugely undervalue Ireland's mineral wealth potential. Eamon Ryan, being unable to tear up this agreement, chose instead to change the taxation arrangement on extracted fossil fuels more in favour of the State.

Even in the departments where we were meant to have control, progress on legislation was, we felt, far too slow. In the Department of the Environment, Heritage and Local Government, John Gormley found that his officials were being less than co-operative in helping to draft key legislation on planning and on climate change.

At Cabinet level, we were coming up against a further obstacle in the form of the Attorney General Paul Gallagher. We weren't aware of him prior to his appointment, but he seems to have been highly regarded in the Law Library. His legal philosophy appeared to be very conservative. To us, it looked as if a greater level of scrutiny was applied to proposed legislation when it emanated from a Green Party source at Cabinet than when it came from another source, with additional reasons often being found as to why such legislation should be proceeded with at a slower pace, if it was proceeded with at all.

The hair-dragging that this constant prevarication brought out in us reminded me of a piece of advice offered by Joe Noonan when he was unwilling to become programme manager: that the most important Cabinet position that the party should seek should be that of Attorney General. It was another lesson, in a long list of lessons, painfully learned.

The issue of incineration of waste was also proving difficult. During negotiations, Fianna Fáil weren't giving much away on the issue. The Green strategy was to undermine the economic viability of incineration. It was agreed that incineration would no longer be the first priority of waste disposal. A commitment to introduce an incineration levy was also agreed. We felt that the put-or-pay clause in the contract agreed by Dublin City Council for the proposed Poolbeg incinerator amounted to a subsidy for the incinerator company, and was against the taxpayers' interest. Without a levy in effect, the State would be giving incineration a further subsidy.

The sanction for this perverse policy had happened during the previous government. It was a source of huge frustration to John Gormley that the existence of this contract, with its probable cost to the taxpayer, was not being taken seriously within the government or by the media.

Political opponents presented the issue of incineration as a matter of local problems for individual Greens. The proposed incinerator for Poolbeg, for instance, was in the heart of John Gormley's Dublin South East constituency, while in Cork South Central I had been dealing for several years with a dual incinerator proposal for Ringaskiddy. In reality, Green waste policy saw incineration as dangerous, outmoded, harmful to the environment and sending all the wrong signals regarding how waste should be dealt with.

As had happened with Lismullen and the M3 motorway decision, attempts were made to pull the rug out from under the Greens before the party had entered government. Dublin City Council through its City Manager had entered into a pre-contract arrangement with the US company Covanta two days before John Gormley became Minister for the Environment to develop an incinerator at Poolbeg.

The contract finalised in September 2008 contained a 'put in pay' clause that committed the Irish taxpayer to pay for waste not provided, thereby committing Dublin local authorities to produce more waste to feed the incinerator.

As Minister, John Gormley was prevented from intervening because Poolbeg remained in the planning and licensing process. The Environmental Protection Agency increased John Gormley's discomfort further by issuing a draft waste licence for Poolbeg in September 2007. Within a year, the agency would issue a full licence, albeit one with strict conditions attached.

That summer, a local difficulty caused more problems, as well as further undermining the environmental credibility of the Greens. Since the closure of Irish Ispat steel plant on Haulbowline Island in Cork Harbour, a toxic waste dump was leaving an unacceptable legacy. On becoming Minister for the Environment, John Gormley had made the clean-up of the site a priority. During his term of office, €35 million would be spent for this purpose.

The contractor and their sub-contractors began a dispute with the Department of the Environment. The contract stipulated payment by volume of material removed. The Department believed that the work was progressing too slowly, and that most of material being removed was inert, 'bulking up' loads that were expensively paid for by the Department.

The sub-contractor maintained that a German laboratory had analysed a sample from the island and found high concentrations of the substance Chromium 6, a carcinogen that had seeped into public consciousness because of the film Erin Brockovich. The laboratory had analysed a sample that had been supplied to it by the contractor, but was not involved in extracting the sample from the island. This seems to have escaped the interest of those who ran with this story, which caused considerable public disquiet.

John Gormley released all of the monitoring results that under previous governments had been kept secret. Green discomfort was made worse by the persistent goading by Labour Party representatives in the area, particularly as Greens considered that the Labour Party was responsible for the situation due to the tawdry deal that it had entered into whilst in government to sell Irish Steel, thus unnecessarily prolonging the life of the plant and increasing the amount of toxic dumping that occurred there.

The most destabilising aspect of the new Cabinet was the decision of Seamus Brennan to step down from the Cabinet. By this stage he was quite ill from cancer, and was unable to carry out his ministerial function. Nevertheless, his absence meant that a supportive presence, one who had worked hard to bring the coalition in being, was no longer there. He sadly lost his battle for life in July 2008. Where he would subsequently be missed was as a calming influence, and as an experienced hand who would have better pre-empted many of the difficulties that were later to arise.

Relationships at Cabinet level at this stage were generally good. Both John and Eamon were receiving plaudits for how they were tackling ministerial office. We realised, of course, that much of this was soft-soaping, although John continued to be viewed with some suspicion.

With Eamon there seemed to be genuine delight amongst Fianna Fáilers, which worried many in the Green Party. 'Going native' was one the biggest fears we had on entering government. Eamon, while doing a good job, was seen as being too well liked by Fianna Fáil.

Working relationships between the Green ministers and other Cabinet Ministers varied. Despite a constant disagreement with her policy on health, relations with Mary Harney were quite good. John Gormley would regularly quote her comment to him that the worst day in government is better than the best day in opposition. Micheál Martin, Willie O'Dea and Eamon O'Cuiv were the Cabinet members who seemed most positively disposed to proposals made by the two Green ministers. Dermot Ahern and Martin Cullen were the ministers with whom the most difficult relations existed.

Internally, each Monday, the Green Party Cabinet Ministers met to prepare for the following day's Cabinet meeting. Meeting with them would be Donal Geoghegan, John's advisor Ryan Meade and Eamon's advisor Sue Duke. Occasionally others would also attend – Bríd McGrath, Liam Reid, David Healy, Aoife Ní Lochlainn, and whenever economic issues were to the fore I also attended.

In addition to that, each Tuesday morning in advance of the Cabinet meeting there was a 30-minute meeting between the Taoiseach and John Gormley. In advance of those meetings, members of the Green parliamentary party would be given red folders, corresponding with the spokesperson roles, of decisions to be made at Cabinet. While this wasn't the extent of documentation received by members of the Cabinet, it did mean that Green TDs and Senators were better informed than any Fianna Fáil back-bencher, and more than a few Fianna Fáil Cabinet Ministers.

The Green team of staff and advisors were incredibly busy. This led to unanticipated and unexpected problems within the party. Local councillors and other party members were finding it hard to get responses from Green Party Ministers or their offices. The infrastructure put in place for responding to enquires was not strong enough; the leadership was losing touch with the rank and file, which was leading to a degree of simmering discontent.

Meanwhile, the preoccupation with Bertie Ahern leaving and Brian Cowen taking his place meant that little or no attention was being given to the Lisbon Treaty referendum. Given the difficulties experienced in approving the Treaty of Nice, the near indifference this was given, not only from the government but also for the pro-EU opposition parties, was to prove inexcusable. The referendum was resoundingly defeated. It was the biggest vote ever cast in an EU referendum, with a 'No' vote in excess of any 'Yes' vote previously recorded. Within weeks of becoming Taoiseach, Brian Cowen's honeymoon had come to a crashing end.

While this debacle was a headache for the government, it didn't ignite a schism within the Green Party. The reasons for the 'No' vote, in retrospect, seemed obvious. There was a lack of identification between citizens and the concept and the purpose of the European Union – a very real democratic deficit, deepened by the lack of democratic structures within the European Union. It was clear that a vote of citizens in most other EU countries would produce a similar result.

In the life of most governments such an event would be seen as a humiliation that would frame a term of office and would be difficult to overcome. In the light of what was to follow this reverse would become the least of the government's, and consequently the country's, worries.

6 | Guaranteed To Fail

The Oireachtas summer break seemed especially welcome that year. We had experienced what we thought were the events that would prove to be the turning point in the life of any government: a change of leadership at the top, coupled with the humiliating loss of a European referendum – circumstances that surely couldn't be repeated. Things couldn't get any worse, or so we thought.

Economically, there were many warning signs. From the start of 2008, tax receipts were falling dramatically, largely on foot of a slowdown in new construction. This was being particularly felt through vastly reduced stamp duty receipts and VAT returns. Also worrying was a slowdown in corporation tax payments. None of this was particularly surprising. Nor were we in any way convinced by the repetitive chants of Fianna Fáil ministers that the economy was going to experience a soft landing. We were aware that these factors were going to make the economy, and more particularly the public finances, a lot harder to manage. However, in addition to this there were also external, international factors that would soon turn what had been a bad leak in the roof into a raging torrent.

Looking back now it is surprising how little discussion on banking occurred prior to September 2008, whether within the Oireachtas, at the Cabinet level, or within our parliamentary party. Huge assumptions were made that the regulation and supervision of banks was something that was quite properly outside of political control. Regulation of banks should be independent, should be impartial and must be outside of political interference. Unfortunately, in ensuring that political inference wouldn't be possible, a system of non-regulation seems to have evolved.

As the Green Party's spokesperson on Finance, I remember spending time some years previously in Committee Room 4 in Leinster House 2000, the adjoining building to Leinster House where the committee rooms are located, discussing the report stage of the Central Bank and the Irish Financial Services Regulatory Authority Bill. At that stage, the debate seemed almost esoteric, centring around the prudential/supervision role or the area of consumer protection.

I also have a clear recollection of the last act of Charlie McCreevy as Minister for Finance, prior to his appointment as a European Commissioner. He announced dozens of appointments to the supervisory committees of the newly established Irish Financial Services Regulatory Authority, or 'IFSRA'. This was announced as being a political departure, with McCreevy making a virtue of the fact that rather than handpicking and selecting, as was his and Fianna Fáil's wont, these appointments were self-selected from within the financial services industry itself!

As international events unfolded there was at first indifference, followed by complacency, which eventually led to panic. The collapse and eventual nationalisation of the Northern Rock Building Society in the UK was seen here as a local difficulty being dealt with there. The fact that it was a building society, that the state of the property market was at the root of its problems and that it had a considerable number of Irish investors didn't seem to register in Ireland. As a news event it wasn't even discussed, nor was it talked about within our parliamentary party, although most likely it was spoken of at Cabinet level. At best, it formed the basis of small, informal conversations for most of us.

In March 2008 we learned of the fate of the Bear Stearns Bank in the United States, which specialised in securitisation – the sale of asset-based securities, mainly sub-prime mortgages. We were learning a new language as well as undertaking a literal crash course in new financial services products. The eventual fire-sale of this bank to JP Morgan Chase was seen in Ireland as an American problem being dealt with by the Americans. The continuing warning theme of a deteriorating property market, which had been artificially inflated by financial institutions, continued to be lost on Ireland.

As the Dáil and the Seanad were rising there was some activity in Irish banks, none of which was publicly or politically visible. Sean Quinn, the much-lauded businessman, was selling a 10% stake in Anglo Irish Bank, in which he was a major shareholder. Much later it was learned that this was part of an exercise to artificially inflate that bank's share price.

Early September saw the political parties hold their now regular 'think-in's in advance of the resumption of the Dáil and the Seanad. The Green Party held ours in Tralee. We were in good heart: many of our candidates in the coming summer's local elections were present, and the mood was that we were achieving in government.

While we were meeting, further bad news arrived from the United States. The US government had decided to nationalise the 'Fannie Mae' and 'Freddie Mac' agencies that had been established to help low-income households get housing. Once again, the words 'property' and 'banks' were flashing like neon lights, and still little attention was being paid to an impending crisis.

Then on September 15th came the news, again from the US, that the largest financial institution to date had collapsed, and for the very same reasons that had been signposted by the Bear Stearns collapse a number a months earlier. The Lehman Brothers collapse made everyone sit up and take notice. The globalised nature of the Irish economy meant that the catching of a cold in the US meant that pneumonia would follow in Ireland.

The regular subsequent mentions of the Lehman Brothers collapse as the prime causal factor in the Irish economy's difficulties, particularly by Fianna Fáil spokespersons, would eventually evoke public derision. Lehman Brothers was not the cause of economic collapse in the Irish economy and Irish banking, but it did help to make a bad situation worse. The announcement about Lehman Brothers threw the world's markets into a panic, and started a domino effect that was particularly strongly felt in Ireland.

Lehman was followed in quick succession by Merrill Lynch, and then by the world's largest insurance group, AIG. Panic was enveloping the world's markets. In Ireland, this panic was becoming pervasive. In official circles nothing was being said or done by those who were meant to provide confidence under these circumstances. The Central Bank and the Office of the Financial Regulator not only seemed ill-equipped to deal with the crisis, but did not seem to be able to explain what was happening, why it was happening and what the appropriate response was.

Into this vacuum, others voices emerged. David McWilliams, a by now well-established commentator and pundit, was someone whose opinion was particularly valued. He made contact with John Gormley, and proposed what policy options should be considered. Simultaneously, McWilliams was also meeting with the Minister for Finance,

Brian Lenihan. These meetings he controversially described in a book *Follow The Money* and in newspapers in October 2009. In these accounts, McWilliams is quite clear that he advocated what he described as a 'nuclear option' – that the government should guarantee the banks.

He was subsequently to argue that the bank guarantee was not what he proposed. However, in a newspaper article published on September 28th 2008 with the headline 'State guarantee can avert depression', he wrote:

> The only option is to guarantee 100 per cent of all depositors/creditors in the Irish banking system. This guarantee does not extend to shareholders, who will have to live with the losses they have suffered. However, it applies to everyone else.
>
> The beauty of guaranteeing deposits is that you use no money – not a penny. Instead, the government is using its sovereign credit as the country with Europe's lowest debt/GDP level to restore confidence in the system. The civil service view appears to be that such a guarantee would subject Ireland to the risk that people withdraw money, disbelieving the state.
>
> But this would not happen. Some €350 billion of the total €500 billion is held by Irish people, so we won't move our cash. In addition, the €150 billion owned by foreigners would simply become like an Irish government paper.

What he wrote in this article coincided precisely with what he saying to Brian Lenihan and John Gormley. Together with the Taoiseach Brian Cowen, a great deal of discussion was taking place in and around the Cabinet with regards to the feasibility of this option.

The options were limited, and each contained a high degree of risk. The Department of Finance commissioned a report from Merrill Lynch outlining what these options were. This was subsequently reported as warning the government not to proceed with the bank guarantee option. It did no such thing. The report was carefully couched in the language of consultancy. It examined each option, stated how each was likely to play out, and highlighted the advantages and disadvantages of each approach. Its view on a bank guarantee was no more negative than its view on other options.

It's worth bearing in mind what those options were. Option one was the truly nuclear option – let the banks fail and live with the consequences. The consequences of so doing were unknown, and as such unmanageable. Extensive uncertainty had already been created, and the policy response chosen could not afford to add to this, which was why the nuclear option could never seriously be considered. The failure of banks would have had a domino effect throughout the economy. In all likelihood there would have been a run on banks, many of which may not have even opened, and there would be a stop on a huge number of payments, including wages.

The only feasible option other than a bank guarantee was the insurance option advocated by some in the UK, and later by Timothy Geithner, the US Secretary of the Treasury in the new Obama administration. That option also carried risk, not least being the payment of a substantial up-front premium with little guarantee such a risk could be underwritten anyway.

None of these policy options address the concern within the general public as to why an Irish government should take responsibility for private banking debt. It galls, it still galls.

The political reality is that the Irish State licenses banks and is responsible for their regulation. Failure in these areas creates a responsibility, at least for some of these debts. The more obvious reality is that the banks borrow from the same sources as the Irish government. Internationally reneging on any of the debt within Ireland would not just be seen as a failure of Irish Banks, but as a failure of the Irish State, which would make it all but impossible for the State to borrow additional money, or at least to do so at sustainable rates of interest. The truth of the matter continues to be that Ireland is part of a multi-national currency governed outside of the State, which limits the independence of its fiscal decision making.

The degree of prior discussion and debate around the bank guarantee undermines a lot of the mythology of the meeting that occurred in Government Buildings on September 29th. As far as John Gormley was concerned, the use and implementation of a bank guarantee had been *de facto* government policy since the previous Saturday, September 26th.

Of course, the circumstances around that meeting are not without causes for concern. The chief executive and chairpersons of the country's two largest banks – Bank of Ireland and AIB – sought a meeting with the Minister for Finance and the Taoiseach. Within banking circles, it was by then known, or at least being admitted, that Anglo Irish Bank had severe liquidity problems, if not dangerously close to insolvency. The bankers had sought and were attending this meeting out of their obvious self-interest. AIB was thought to be particularly exposed to an Anglo collapse.

It has been speculated that the insolvency of Anglo Irish Bank was known to those of us in government. It wasn't. It was feared by us for certain, but every piece of official advice we were receiving was telling us that Anglo could achieve viability.

The Cabinet was briefed that the meeting was taking place, and told to be prepared for a possible Cabinet meeting later that night. Any decision would need to have been made before the markets opened on the following morning. As the night progressed, the rest of the Cabinet individually decided that a meeting wasn't likely to take place.

By this stage, the idea of a bank guarantee would only have been discussed briefly, and not at any great depth within the Cabinet. More detail would have been discussed between Brain Cowen, Brian Lenihan and John Gormley. I have no recollection of the idea being discussed beforehand by the Green parliamentary party. When announced, it was something to which, as the party's spokesperson on Finance, I would have had to react.

In the early hours of September 29th, Brian Cowen and Brian Lenihan agreed with the bankers that the Government should seek to put into place an all-encompassing bank guarantee. The Taoiseach agreed that Cabinet assent would be required through the holding of an incorporeal meeting of the Cabinet, seeking out Government Ministers individually. This proved to be difficult, as many Ministers seemed to be inaccessible.

John Gormley proved extremely difficult to contact. His phone wasn't responding. It was decided to send his Garda driver to him. It was 2.00 a.m., and having had no previous update he had gone to bed. This was subsequently represented as John being asleep at the wheel, a further negligent act from not having attended the meeting. This was more mythology. John had already been intimately involved in the *de facto* policy decision that an all-encompassing bank guarantee, if required, should be put in place. Those who attended the meeting in Government Buildings – the Taoiseach and the Minister for Finance – were the only members of the

Cabinet who needed to be there. Ultimately though, as a Cabinet decision was required to implement the policy on a bank guarantee, whether physical or incorporeal, John had influence on whether or not the policy was to be proceeded with. When John Gormley contacted Brian Cowen on that fateful night, he asked directly whether the Cabinet was being asked to consider the McWilliams option, to which he was given a clear and direct answer of 'yes'.

The Cabinet decision was announced, and when the international markets opened that morning there seemed to be a welcome for the policy initiative. That welcome was far from universal. The Irish media seized on a €400 billion figure that would be the cost to the State should the guarantee be called on in its entirety. This risk came to equate in the public mind with the direct cost, an argument that could never be subsequently won. Whatever significant cost would be realised, that higher potential cost would always rank within the public's consciousness.

Within the European Union, there was widespread unhappiness that the Irish government had embarked on the guarantee without consultation. The UK government was furious; its Chancellor Alistair Darling did not hold back in his denunciation of the guarantee. There existed in the UK a legitimate fear that funds would move from the UK into Ireland because of this announcement. The views of the British government were replicated within the British financial press, which then began a sustained campaign of negative reporting of and towards the Irish economy.

At first, the guarantee announcement seemed to be having a positive effect. Additional money was coming into the country and its banks for investment here, but this was an effect that was soon dissipated as other European countries began to put in place variants of guarantees in their countries.

The narrative developing was that the problem was largely an Irish one. While we had made things more difficult for ourselves, problems of a similar nature were being experienced in many other countries. On October 1st, the United States modified its $700 billion bailout plan for banks, issued a few short weeks earlier, to extend bank guarantees to $250,000 per account. On October 2nd, Greece replicated Ireland's bank guarantee. By October 7th, several other European countries including Austria, Belgium, Denmark, the Netherlands and Spain introduced similar guarantees. Britain increased its bank guarantee on the same day.

At the same time, several key financial institutions in other countries were experiencing pressure. The Dutch government nationalised Fortis bank, a bank that had been a key investor in helping to develop a now stillborn Post Bank in Ireland. In Germany, the government had already been forced into a revision of its bailout plan for Hypo Real Estate. Iceland by this time had stepped into the abyss. Its currency dropped by 30% against the Euro. They introduced emergency legislation to nationalise two banks and to rescue a third. Within days, its Financial Services Authority was suspending market trading on six Icelandic banks.

On October 8th, the British government made £25 billion available to a range of its financial institutions including Abbey, Barclays, HBOS, HSBC Bank plc, Lloyds TSB, Nationwide Building Society, Royal Bank of Scotland and Standard Chartered as part of a bank rescue package. Later, the BBC economics editor Robert Peston reported that Royal Bank of Scotland and HBOS were – on that day – only hours away from being unable to open for business.

Also on October 8th, the European Central Bank, the Bank of England, the Federal Reserve, the Bank of Canada, the Swedish Riksbank and the Swiss National Bank all announced simultaneous cuts of 0.5% to their base rates. They were followed by the Central Bank of the People's Republic of China. There were significant losses on stock markets worldwide. That night, the Central Bank of Iceland abandoned its attempt to peg the Icelandic Króna to the Euro. By the following morning, it was floating at three times the hoped-for level.

In Japan, Yamato Life filed for bankruptcy. The Russian Parliament passed a loan of $36 billion gained from global oil sales to its banks, particularly Rosselkhozbank, the bank that provided credit to its agricultural sector. The US government placed funds into banks by taking equity interests in them. The action mirrored those of the British government, and amounted to partial nationalisation.

By October 12th, the words and actions of the European Central Bank in effect underpinned the Irish bank guarantee throughout the Eurozone area. By the weekend, the G7 nations, at their meeting in Washington, pledged to 'support systemically important financial institutions and prevent their failure'. Such was the economic environment in which Ireland found itself, and such were the constraints under which we, as a nation and as a government, were placed and continue to be bound.

***

The legislative response to the Irish bank guarantee was the Credit Institutions (Financial Support) Bill 2008. It was introduced into Dail Éireann on September 30th, passing all stages in one day. The Government's position was supported by Fine Gael and by Sinn Féin. Labour chose to take a deliberately contrarian line without offering a clear alternative. On the following day, the Seanad sat into the morning hours to finalise the legislation. I got to say the following in my second-stage speech:

> At this ungodly hour of the morning we need to ask ourselves how we got to where we are now. It has resulted from a combination of factors, mainly the global situation and partially the situation in which we find ourselves in this country. We are in a position, not unlike that in other jurisdictions, to present to other countries an alternative and a response that is unique. The Government has come up with a response that is in the Irish interest and reflects the reality of the economy. That said, we are in epoch-making times. Many of us may question the epoch we are about to make, but we must live with the reality of where we are because of a combination of factors, partially global but many brought about by irresponsible practices. The fact that there were those irresponsible practices must be acknowledged by this Chamber and those of us in public life who recognise that we live in a world where the global situation is having too much of an effect on our everyday lives.
>
> The reality of what we are proposing is that the Government is choosing a response that what is local and indigenous is what we need to protect in the first instance. The uncertainty of the global economic climate means we have to take a course of action that whatever economic activity we need to protect, enhance and promote in the future must in the first place be based in the economy. We have come through an economic climate globally where we have been led to believe the shifting sands of what can be produced in terms of economic wealth do not require long-term sustainability. We know this is not the case. There is a responsibility, which

we must live up to. We must recognise that the financial systems internationally and what has been practised in this country and elsewhere throughout the European Union have been based on a mythology and dishonesty such that people believe wealth can be created out of nothing.

What is being proposed by the Government is that the State needs to take in hand, by way of an underwriting agreement, that the future of the economy is based on the fact that, being the only body that can bring about a guarantee of stability, at least in the short term, it is putting in place a financial system that will be more sustainable in the future than that which we have had in the recent past. We can look at others to make accusations, the United States being the pre-eminent economy on which we have relied too heavily to bring about an unreality as to where we are at.

Ultimately, the Bill asks questions not only of our financial system but where we as legislators can bring our people in terms of a new economic reality. I am satisfied that the safeguards in place here are better than those being proposed by other countries. The reality of the United States vote, which many of us were watching while we were waiting to start this debate, whereby a toxic debt that is not redeemable in the short term is being bought and where our nearest jurisdiction, the United Kingdom, is buying up financial institutions as and when they are likely to go out of business, is not one that a small economy such as ours can face up to. We are proposing a measure that is bold in its intent, but which can be more successful in the medium and long term than what I would argue are the other panic reactions of larger and more established economies. We *should take the courage of that conviction and bring it forward and learn the lessons of the economic success we have gained during the past ten years. Otherwise, we will just be repeating the mistakes and replicating other economic failures we have seen throughout the world. I encourage Members to follow that example.*

I accept now that there is much that was naïve in what I was saying, but some of these points were essential truths, from the international nature of the banking crisis to the need to produce a response that fitted Irish circumstances – circumstances that were made worse in Ireland by the reckless lending by Irish banks, and the failure of the State to regulate the industry in any way whatsoever. Final votes on the bill in the Seanad took place at 7.45 a.m. after an all-night sitting, designed to have certainty before the international markets opened on the following morning. As we streamed out into the morning light, a number of us, including Déirdre de Búrca and myself, were confronted with a Morning Ireland reporter who expected us to be coherent about an issue that, after sixteen hours in the chamber, had scrambled all our minds.

It was the defining event in the life of the government. The existence of the guarantee became the shorthand for everything that was wrong with what the government was doing in terms of economic policy. While there was no escaping this analysis, it was an analysis that was defined largely in retrospect. The guarantee at the time seemed to hold a number of attractions. It required no initial outlay, although the potential risk of €400 billion should the guarantee be called at once by all participating institutions was soon being presented as an actual cost. Restricting the institutions participating in the facility to only Irish registered banks was meant to reduce this risk, but as the most spectacularly failing banks were Irish registered banks this would soon be a moot point.

This too would also prove to be a delusion. The daily liquidity needs of Irish banks were being met by colossal injections from the European Central Bank, with that giving the ECB a determining role in what policy decisions would be or could be taken in relation to Irish banks. The dichotomy of whether the nature of the problems of Irish banking was one of liquidity or solvency was something of a false dichotomy. A large-scale, all-embracing bank guarantee would have been required to resolve the problem, whether of liquidity or of solvency. There was no doubt subsequently that the banks lied about their situation that evening in government buildings, and that particularly the situation of Anglo Irish Bank was being grossly misrepresented. What wasn't known at the time of the guarantee, and what couldn't have been know then, was the scale of the debts the banks had, and the risks of greater debts to come, requiring a degree of recapitalisation that was to be constantly revised in subsequent years and that still defies credibility.

The scope of those debts became apparent as a series of stress tests by Irish regulatory authorities, and later by their European counterparts, revealed the extent of the recapitalisation needs of Irish banks that had to be met by a combination of direct payment of new capital, the taking of State equity stakes and, in the case of Anglo Irish, the issuing of promissory notes. The scale of the amounts involved, when revealed, shocked everyone. It was felt that this had to be grasped, and there was no expectation that further, larger amounts would later be needed.

A bill for the nationalisation of Anglo Irish Bank had been prepared to coincide with the legislation on the bank guarantee. It was decided to sit on that legislation for a number of months. That was a mistake. Anglo should not have been part of the bank guarantee. It should have been nationalised immediately. Such a move would not have absolved the State from having to meet most of the debts built up by Anglo Irish, but could have given more freedom to have dealt in a pre-emptive way with subordinate bondholders. At the end of the day, that approach may not have worked either as with everything else the agreement and the co-operation of the European Central Bank might not have been forthcoming, and that co-operation was and remains essential.

The putting in place of the bank guarantee and the initial re-capitalisation requirements began, in earnest, a process of questioning those who had been charged with regulating the financial institutions. This questioning at first was muted. There seemed to exist some unwritten rule that senior public servants should not be overtly questioned in public. The position of the Chief Executive of the Office of the Financial Regulator, Patrick Neary, seemed untenable. The opposition Finance spokespersons, Fine Gael's Richard Bruton and Labour's Joan Burton, seemed slow to say so. I was the first Finance spokesperson to call for his resignation.

When that resignation eventually came, the way it was handled started a chain of events that further undermined public confidence. The board of IFSRA, as Patrick Neary's employers, chose to offer a severance package over and above statutory requirements, with a considerable sweetener for vacating the Chief Executive position early. The decision was made by IFSRA, an independent body, and couldn't be overridden by the Government or the Minister for Finance. That did not stop the impression being formed by the general public that it was officially approved and sanctioned; that, at the highest level of government and administration, failure was and would be rewarded. It was a pattern that would be repeated far too frequently with subsequent resignations.

The crisis surrounding those events released a torrent of reports from sources whose companies were intimately involved with the same events even as they were unfolding globally. Consulting companies like Merrill Lynch, Price Waterhouse Coopers and Rothschilds were commissioned by the government through the Department of Finance to work out an Irish government response. Many of these reports, while analysing the situation and assessing options, rarely gave hard proposals on concrete actions that should be followed.

In the Green Party, it would be fair to say that we were being overwhelmed with the amount of information being created. In the earlier part of the crisis we accepted too much on trust, and left the detail to be presented by others. These cataclysmic events caused a dramatic change of approach on our part. For the guarantee itself, John had been directly involved. At Cabinet level, Eamon Ryan took that responsibility on to a greater degree, and began taking more responsibility on the economic policy questions. Up to then my role as party spokesperson was to work with our Cabinet Ministers and to react to events. From then on we insisted and demanded greater prior consultation. This resulted in more regular meetings with department officials, and with those who were being contracted on behalf of the government. As Minister for Finance, Brian Lenihan showed that he was willing to be more informal in relation to Cabinet protocol and consult more widely.

Now, years later, the question can be better asked as to what should have been done then. I remain convinced that a wide-scale bank guarantee had to be put in place. Legitimate questions surround whether all Irish financial institutions should have been included, and whether all debtor categories should be considered, but the guarantee itself was unavoidable.

The added government debt being created through the bank guarantee, most immediately through re-capitalisation, and the already badly deteriorating tax returns, was creating a demand for the next budget to be brought forward. The Minister for Finance acceded to these demands, believing it to be a decisive action that would help restore confidence in the global markets. It soon proved to be another major mistake in the life of the government.

7 | A Budget Too Soon

The decision to bring the 2009 budget forward to October 2008 meant that budget preparations became extremely rushed. The scale of the adjustment required in that budget, which had to be significant, was relatively quickly agreed. The Green Party's initial approach was to spread the unavoidable pain over a long time period to make that pain more bearable, but the initial tranche had to be significant.

Wider areas of disagreement existed over how the adjustment would be spread between increases in taxation and cuts in public expenditure. The Greens believed and argued that the bias should be weighted towards greater taxation. We wished to see an earlier introduction of a carbon tax. We wanted increases in capital taxation. We wished that the unsustainable and unfair tax reliefs would be phased out on a quicker basis. We were far less nervous about increasing tax rates, especially at the higher levels of pay, than our partners in government. The Department of Finance had and has continued to have an attachment to not increasing the highest marginal rate of tax. We believed that taxation policy should be determined by the effective rates of tax, which for many high-income earners remained relatively low.

The Department of Finance proposed and wanted to introduce an income levy. We felt that this was a blunt instrument, but it did have the advantage of dealing with gross income that would be impossible for higher-income earners to avoid. Having lost the argument on the income levy rather than higher tax rates, the Greens' attention turned to how the income levy could be made fairer. Through these discussions we did succeed in raising the lower threshold and getting more proportionality through the various bands.

We also lost the argument on cuts rather than tax increases. The mindset that has existed and continues to exist in the Department for Finance is that each budget in a period of readjustment should have a bias of more cuts and less increases in taxation. For a first adjustment budget it was probably best we did. The theory is to try and keep as much money in people's pockets as possible so that it can be spent in helping to regenerate the economy. The difficulty over the longer term is that a series of spending cuts reduces the ability of the government to stimulate the economy through its spending. This became another area of difficulty in a growing list of government difficulties.

Despite government expenditure being cut in many areas, there were also some increases in social welfare payments, in disability payments and for carers. To meet the cost of this, savings were achieved by changing eligibility criteria, increasing contributions and introducing new lower rate categories such as for the first time unemployed. Child benefit payments were to be stopped at 18 years of age. Rent supplement, as much a subsidy for landlords as it was a means of housing assistance, were dramatically reduced.

The State pension would be increased by €7 a week, but it was from that sector of Irish society that the biggest controversy surrounding the rushed budget would eventually come. The extension of the free medical cards to all citizens over the age of 70 was a politically cute, badly thought through and horribly administered, scheme. Devised, so the story went, a number of years previously on the back of an envelope, it was introduced through a scheme that gave doctors a higher participant rate than the general medical card scheme.

As Minister for Health, Mary Harney and her officials wanted to correct that imbalance. It was right that they wanted to do so. However, the way in which it was proposed to do it brought the government into further disrepute with the electorate. As it was explained to us by the Department of Health, the vast majority of people over 70 would retain their medical cards; the main effect was that doctors would be paid less. When we learned, subsequent to the budget speech, of the income levels at which the means test for entitlement to the new medical cards would apply we were furious. The controversy caused by the move grew in the days following the budget.

Before that, however, the budget speech itself was to cause difficulty. On finishing his speech, Brian Lenihan, with his call to patriotic action, was met with a tribal reaction by Fianna Fáil back-benchers, who stood en masse to give him a standing ovation. Green ministers and TDs responded in kind, partly out of instinct, but also out of an awareness that not to have done so would have been interpreted in a particular way. As a senator I sat in the upper circle of the Dáil chamber. I stayed sitting, believing that this ovation was an utterly inappropriate reaction that would come back to haunt us.

By that stage we were aware that this budget would only be first in a series of difficult budgets, a series that would affect the cycle of the government and would run to the next election and beyond.

Being smug about the most difficult budget in decades seemed bad enough, but the exhibition of grey power that followed threw the government into a panic. A huge protest by pensioners outside the gates of Leinster House meant that the measure could not proceed as proposed. Independent TDs, such as Finian McGrath, who had been supporting the government, began to break ranks. Fianna Fáil had its first casualty when Joe Behan TD voted against the budget. The Green parliamentary party went into an emergency session, the first of many such meetings in the life of this government. At that meeting we talked seriously about whether the Green Party should leave the government. Paul Gogarty was particularly agitated, arguing that our reaction had been too little, too late. And he was right.

Why didn't we leave? There were several questions that we asked ourselves. Knowing that leaving government would not cause an immediate general election, would it really bring about a policy change for the better? In a minority Fianna Fáil government, it would not. What the Green Party could do, though, was try to influence changes in policy approach. In government we could influence; outside of government we could not.

However, with this, and at each subsequent point of considering whether or not to remain in government, we were charged with being concerned primarily with self-interest, while we believed that having entered government we should see that responsibility through. More damaging was the growing belief that the Greens being in government had caused the recession. We were certainly dealing with the results of the recession – the worst economic crisis in the history of the State – but the causal factors that had created that recession had occurred prior to the Greens coming into government.

It was decided that Mary White and Déirdre de Búrca would go to the plinth at Leinster House, meet the media, and state that the Greens wanted to see this measure reversed. In the end, the new income levels were raised so high that it made a nonsense of what was being proposed.

The Greens did succeed in having one revenue-raising change introduced. In this budget, and legislated for in the subsequent Finance Bill, was a €200-a-year charge on benefit-in-kind parking in the city centre areas of the country's major cities. It was a measure that would have largely affected civil and public servants, but also many private-sector employees, as well as TDs, Senators and Ministers. Somehow, even though legislated for, the measure was never implemented.

In the round, it was an ill-considered budget. It was a budget that wasn't properly thought out. It was a budget that failed to address the wider issues, and in a number of months it would have to be revisited.

***

In December the document 'The Smart Economy' was published. A detailed document meant to inspire confidence in a series of actors from investors to important partner institutions such as the European Commission and the European Central Bank, there was much in its contents that derived from Green Party thinking, as this excerpt from its introduction shows:

> The Smart Economy has, at its core, an exemplary research, innovation and commercialisation ecosystem. The objective is to make Ireland an innovation and commercialisation hub in Europe – a country that combines the features of an attractive home for innovative R&D-intensive multinationals while also being a highly

attractive incubation environment for the best entrepreneurs in Europe and beyond. This will be the successful formula for the next phase of the development of the Irish economy and for delivering quality and well-paid jobs.

The Smart Economy is a 'Green Economy' in that it recognises the interrelated challenges of climate change and energy security. It involves the transition to a low-carbon economy and recognises the opportunities for investment and jobs in clean industry. The core of this Green New Deal is a move away from fossil-fuel based energy production through investment in renewable energy and increased energy efficiency to reduce demand, wastage and costs.

This sustainable approach to economic development complements the core strength of our economy in the use of natural resources in the agriculture, forestry, fisheries, tourism and energy sectors. It recognises that our manufacturing industries are already relatively clean and green in the low level of resource inputs they use and environmental outputs they create. It will allow us develop a digital services export economy which will only require a high speed broadband network, a renewable electricity supply and our own ingenuity to succeed.

It was a document that sought to address the difficulties that the economy was then experiencing, with an eye on the growth potential of the medium-term future. It also sought to lay down some principles on how such a future might be defined.

The difficulty in speaking or writing down such language is that the document was underpinned by economic growth projections that were totally unrealistic. It was suggested by the document that the Irish economy would grow on average by 4.5% each year for the following 4 years. 4.5% growth was an unrealistic expectation in 2007, and now we can see that it was fantasy. The Green Party should never have agreed to such projected growth targets. In a crisis-management situation, the ball can get dropped. Through the prism of time it is easier to identify the arguments that should have been made, or made more forcefully.

8 | NAMA GUBU Revisited?

The initial stress testing of Irish banks and financial institutions covered by the bank guarantee revealed enormous amounts of toxic debt on their balance sheets. It seemed clear to the Government that an asset-management approach was needed, and that the State had to be the agency to remove toxic assets from the banks' balance sheets, sit on those assets for a considerable period of time and get better value for those assets in the long term after a hoped-for upturn.

Economist Peter Bacon, long favoured by Fianna Fáil governments, produced what seemed to be an 'off the shelf' approach. His National Asset Management Agency proposal provoked a number of suspicious reactions. A kneejerk response was that this was a lifejacket for builders and developers. The media reported an anecdote of developers together in Spain toasting the suggestion of NAMA as the answer to their prayers.

The opposition parties, when asked how they would approach this issue, produced broadly similar proposals. Fine Gael proposed a bad bank linked to a Bank for National Recovery. The Labour Party proposed an Asset Recovery Trust (ART), which to all intents and purposes was NAMA by another name. The name 'NAMA' was part of the problem. Redolent of GUBU or the discredited Fianna Fáil fundraising arm TACA, it fed conspiratorial theories of

Fianna Fáil looking after its own. Asset management was necessary and unavoidable. How it was to be undertaken also fed conspiracy theories. It was argued that the government would overpay the banks for these debts. Secondary fears were that, once purchased, the debts would then be written off for developer friends.

The gestation of NAMA was far from immediate. There was a gap between it being proposed by Peter Bacon and the production by the Department of Finance of a draft NAMA bill. The draft bill was not, as far as the Green Party was concerned, a government bill. There was much in the bill that we wanted to see, and would insist on being changed. Producing the bill was followed by a long and detailed consultation process.

Those who argued against a large-scale asset-management approach argued that the Irish property market was unlikely to recover for many years, and that having overpaid for assets, the recoupable value of such assets would also diminish and stay shrunken for a very long time.

Other economists began to line up against the proposal. UCD economist Morgan Kelly, who predicted the Irish property collapse more accurately than most, contrasted the approach being taken by the Irish government with the approach that had been taken a number of years previously by the Swedish government in a comparably similar situation.

Karl Whelan, also of UCD, offered a considered and reasoned rationale as to why the Irish government's approach would not be likely to prove effective. Others took a more provocative approach – Constantin Gurdgiev in a stylish way, Brian Lucey from Trinity College, at least to my mind, in a much more obnoxious way.

These arguments and others were causing a great deal of concern among Green Party members. The party organised a number of seminars where each of these economists, with the exception of Morgan Kelly, spoke and answered questions.

A series of meetings were held by our economics policy group, by our National Council and through an *ad hoc* group established solely on the issue of NAMA. Meetings were held at the Hilton Hotel off Charlemont Place. Key party members who drove this process, Gary Fitzgerald and James Nix, were invited to several meetings with Department of Finance officials. It was an unprecedented level of access. Green Party members were among the best informed people in the country on the subject of NAMA and its intricacies. The Green Party's approach to economic policy issues in government was greatly helped by a new advisor taken on in February 2009 by Eamon Ryan in the Department of Energy, Communications and Natural Resources. Stephen O'Connor had worked in the financial services sector, and was a great asset for those of us trying to deal with the complexity of these issues.

As the party's Finance spokesperson, I was attending not only those meetings but also direct briefings with the Department as well as one-to-one meetings with consultants working on developing NAMA. It was a subject that I felt was taking up too much of our time.

In the meantime, Brian Lenihan had taken on Alan Ahearne, who had been based at NUI Galway to become his special economic advisor. Aherne, who had previously worked in the United States with Alan Greenspan and for the World Bank, had been an early and effective critic of the government approach to the banking crisis. By coming on board he had a chance to influence and change policy in a more effective way. As the government's chief economic advisor, he also made himself available to Green Party members to argue what NAMA was and why it was needed.

Another critic, but also from the perspective of wanting to make NAMA work better, was the Trinity College professor Patrick Honohan. Honohan had studied many previous international bank collapses. He proposed a variation on how NAMA would operate, one that introduced an element of risk sharing.

The long consultation on the draft NAMA bill continued throughout 2009. In the summer of that year I was asked to speak at the MacGill Summer School. I was to deliver what I hoped would be a hard-hitting speech criticising people like Patrick Neary and Michael Fingleton, as well as laying down some principles as to how we in the Green Party wanted to see things progress. I was insisting that we would not support the Buggins turn arrangement of senior officials from the Department of Finance slipping into vacant positions in the Financial Regulator's office, and, in the case of the Secretary General of the Department, the expectation of becoming Governor of the Central Bank.

In relation to a new Financial Regulator, we were putting down a further marker that, given the previous incestuous nature of Irish financial services, and the failure of regulation that resulted, we believed that a new regulator should be appointed from outside the jurisdiction.

On the panel with me at MacGill were Patrick Honohan and Alan Dukes, who had been appointed as a State director of Anglo Irish Bank, but who had not yet been appointed as its Chair. I spoke to Patrick Honohan informally at the summer school, and arranged a meeting with him that took place a number of weeks later at Eamon Ryan's ministerial office.

At that meeting we talked about the Honohan variation to NAMA, which we were happy to see included in the draft bill. By pushing his proposal we also advanced his consideration as the next Governor of the Central Bank.

The Honohan variation was one of several changes that the Greens succeeded in including in the legislation before it was brought before the Houses of the Oireachtas. Chief among these was the creation of an 80% windfall tax on the increase in value of land that had been re-zoned. Other important changes related to the structure of NAMA and the extent to which its activities could be and should be open.

Fianna Fáil was particularly unhappy with the Greens' insistence that the legislation should forbid elected representatives from lobbying NAMA in any way. Political interference, in many instances pure corruption in our opinion, had been at the root of many of the planning scandals that had plagued the country. We weren't going to have the same mistake repeated twice. What was especially important to the Greens was the question of a social dividend from NAMA – how to use the strength of NAMA, now as one of the largest development companies in the world, to produce important pieces of social infrastructure. Brian Lenihan promised to produce the appropriate ministerial orders to bring that about.

The process of selecting new State/public-interest directors for financial institutions that were being re-capitalised was a process where the Green Party failed to engage, and should have pursued more strongly. Green nominees such as Richard Douthwaite were not accepted. Ray McSharry, Alan Dukes and Dick Spring did not of themselves represent the wider political spectrum on banking issues. Some, like Frank Daly (former Chair of the Revenue Commissioners) we saw as being suitably independent and impartial. Others were not known to us, and we failed to research their backgrounds.

The fact that some had previously been involved on the boards of these banks, and contributing to the disastrous approaches that were taken, was something to which we should not have agreed.

We had been more concerned with policy than with people. We wanted bank salaries to be capped. We wanted the existing directors on the boards of these institutions to be phased out. While these things were happening, they weren't happening as quickly as we, and the public, would have liked. With NAMA, we insisted in naming people we knew and felt could be trusted to sit on the main board and on advisory panels.

In September of 2009, the last of a series of consultation meetings with Green Party members took place in Athlone. For an issue of such deep controversy, the mood was workmanlike. The meeting decided that its preference would be for the purchase of toxic assets at current market values. That would have made a nonsense of the concept of an asset-management agency, i.e. to buy assets with a haircut but with a small premium from the lowest valuation for the banks, with the expectation that market values would increase over and above such amounts in the medium to long term. What would matter if and when NAMA was established was the size of the haircuts made on the toxic assets of each participating bank, the degree to which the property market would recover and the time period over which that would occur.

Even late in 2009, on the verge of its establishment, NAMA often excited violent reactions. I was asked to take part in the Leviathan political cabaret being held at the Button Factory. The theme of that evening's event was NAMA. Arguing against Constantin Guerdgiev and Peter Mathews, I was placed, not to my pleasure, with Fianna Fáil's

Frank Fahey to argue for NAMA. Economist and regular Leviathan presenter David McWilliams was officiating, but was, in effect, also arguing against NAMA. The audience too was vehemently opposed to NAMA. As the debate ended, an audience member threw two eggs, one of which hit Frank Fahey, the other of which missed me. In retrospect, this seemed to be one of the milder reactions of that evening.

The bank guarantee and NAMA were but two issues whose existence would not permit any rational debate. A third issue was that of a public inquiry into the banks and political decisions relating to the banks. Opposition parties wanted a finger-pointing and finger-wagging exercise. For those parties, a particular emphasis was talked up suggesting that an inquiry was needed into the decision surrounding the bank guarantee, implying sinister intent on the part of the government.

The limits on the ability of Oireachtas committees to compel attendance of witnesses and to make findings of fact (a situation that arose from Supreme Court decisions around the Abbeylara inquiry) would have made such hearings a rather futile exercise. Parliaments in other jurisdictions, like the UK and the US, had managed to balance public accountability with confidentiality. There should have been no reason why this couldn't have happened in Ireland.

There was also a growing clamour for a public inquiry into the banks. Economist Colm McCarthy, who was well thought of by the government, made such a call. As the Greens' Finance spokesperson, transparency was something we believed should happen. My initial call for an inquiry to take place was met by what by now was becoming the stock response of the Taoiseach to most of my interventions – a blank refusal.

Again, it was eventually accepted that a bank inquiry was inevitable. The proposal that was finally engineered was multi-faceted, which I believed had the intent to avoid a public element to the inquiry. A preliminary report would be undertaken by international experts. A Commission of Inquiry with an appointed independent membership would follow, after which public hearings of the Oireachtas Committee on Finance would analyse these reports. Parallel to this process, an internal report was to be undertaken regarding the efficacy of the Department of Finance.

I wasn't happy with this. Rather than clarify the structure, it seemed likely to create further confusion and delay. I went to John Gormley in January 2010 saying that what was being proposed was far from the open, transparent process that I had been advocating as the party's spokesperson. I offered my resignation as spokesperson. John felt that what was announced met what we were looking for. I reluctantly agreed that I would wait to see how they would operate.

We had achieved the holding of an inquiry, as well as a commitment that they would be processed by the end of 2010. The preliminary report by Klaus Regling and Max Watson was encouraging. The later appointment of Finnish civil servant Peter Nyberg as the sole member of a Commission of Inquiry into Banking showed independence, and would raise levels of confidence in the process.

However, the lack of a public element to these inquiries, which were not the Star Chamber hoped for by the opposition parties, limited the extent to which the public could have confidence that the banking sector was being exposed with future accountability taking root.

9 | The Year of Living Dangerously

On New Year's Eve I had sent a jokey text to my friends saying: '2009 will be fine. Trust me, I'm a politician.' It wasn't meant to be taken seriously, but I was soon to realise how wrong I would be.

The year started on a very sad note, with the death after a long illness of Tony Gregory, an iconic figure in Irish politics. Tony's politics wouldn't have been all that close to the Green Party, although he was a noted animal rights campaigner and we got on well with each other. His office was on the same floor of the Leinster House 2000 building as Green Oireachtas members. Many of us had strong personal relations with Tony, and his death removed a supportive presence from the Oireachtas.

The fallout from the October budget spilled into 2009. The protesting pensioners were followed by 100,000 taking to the streets against the general thrust of government policy. 2009 was an election year, with Local and European elections due in June. It was hardly the way the government parties wanted to begin an election year.

Discontent within the Green Party, particularly amongst those least happy with the party's decision to enter into government, had now come to the fore as a result of the budget. Two councillors resigned, Chris O'Leary in Cork and Bronwen Maher in Dublin, in what seemed to be an almost choreographed way. Chris presented his departure in an article in Phoenix magazine as a catalogue of slights he was supposed to have received in Cork. Few of the people that Chris had brought into party, other than family members, left with him. People like Mick Murphy and Ken Walsh directly disagreed with how Chris was presenting his case. Mick Murphy sought to have a clarification printed in Phoenix that the magazine refused to print. Bronwen Maher, who seemed put out that Chris O'Leary had beaten her to a resignation from the party, seemed to raise the ante further. Where Chris resigned to become an independent, at least temporarily, Bronwen went straight from the Greens into Labour. She cited the Green Party as having lost its 'moral compass'. Later, she would appear at a fringe meeting at the English Green Party's annual conference making similar arguments unchallenged.

As a result of these resignations, the party had no local government representation in the two largest cities in the country. Chris's defection had always seemed probable. It's likely that both resignations were fuelled by fears of political survival. There was less support among party members, however, for the actions of Bronwen Maher. Her criticisms were seen to be unfair and far too bitter.

Perversely, an opinion poll that directly followed these resignations showed an increase in Green Party support. It was in line with a trend in opinion polls that consistently showed Green Party support higher than the levels won in the 2007 General Election.

The party still had to prepare for the European elections. The party had performed well in European elections in the past, electing two MEPs twice. The overall reduction in Irish seats, with all Euro-constituencies now limited to three seats in size, made a repeat of this feat far less likely.

In truth, the person in the party most enthusiastic for the European elections was Déirdre de Búrca. Deirdre had long set her sights on a position in Brussels, wanting to be a candidate, and prepared to put the maximum effort into achieving election. The only question that had to be resolved was which constituency was she likely to contest. She had been based in Bray, Wicklow, for a number of years. As a Senator, she had a public office in the town. She had been a county and town councillor there too. Nuala Ahern had been elected twice as a Green MEP for Leinster from a nearby Greystones base. Deirdre was from South County Dublin, and the Dublin Euro-constituency had the stronger, more consistent Green vote. Her preference was to stand there instead.

This created the obvious political difficulty of being seen to turn her back on her Dáil constituency. A number of years previously, Monica Barnes, when a serving Fine Gael TD for Dún Laoghaire, stood as a candidate for the Leinster Euro-constituency. Alan Dukes first stood as a Fine Gael candidate for the Munster Euro-constituency before becoming a TD for Kildare South. While precedents existed, it would still be a hard story to sell.

It also created some friction between John Gormley and Déirdre de Búrca, a relationship that was already fraught. John's view was that proposing Deirdre for the Seanad gave her a strong base for the coming Dáil election, and running for the European Parliament was endangering that. Deirdre's belief was that contesting the European elections was her priority.

Ideally, John would have liked Nessa Childers, a Green councillor in Dún Laoghaire and daughter of former President Erskine Childers, to have been the Green candidate in Dublin, with Deirdre being the candidate in Leinster, giving the party high-profile candidates in two Euro-constituencies.

His hope soon became irrelevant. Nessa Childers announced her intention to resign as a councillor, and stood down from public life for what she cited as 'family reasons'. Those at least were the reasons she gave to me when I met her as Party Chair, after which I thanked her for her service as a party representative. It caused some slight surprise when, a short number of weeks later, she decided to re-enter public life in order to seek the Labour Party nomination for the Leinster Euro-constituency.

This move, coupled with Déirdre de Búrca's insistence on seeking a nomination for the party In Dublin, meant that it was unlikely that the Green Party would contest the Leinster Euro-consistency. The party's electoral task force felt that it was important in terms of national profile that it should contest at least two of the four Euro-constituencies. I was asked to be a candidate for the Munster Euro-constituency, or 'Ireland South' as it had been renamed. It wasn't something I sought, neither was it something that anyone in the party believed was likely to succeed. The logic was that the additional profile I had acquired as Party Chair would help to maximise the national vote of the party.

Selection conventions, endorsements really as their outcomes were not in question, were organised in Dublin and Cork. The events doubled up as members meetings to discuss the ongoing fallout from the budget. The mood at both meetings was uncertain, but for the most part continued to be supportive of the party leadership.

The party's annual convention was organised for March of that year in Wexford. John Gormley's instinct, usually unerring, predicted trouble ahead. He had come to believe that the scale of what was facing the country, added to what was yet to come, required normal politics be suspended and a National Government to be put in place.

He had an opinion poll taken that indicated that many voters were prepared to accept that happening. He wanted to allude to this in his leader's address, but was warned against it, and delivered a muted reference instead. Even this reference was treated indifferently, if predictability, by the leaders of the opposition parties.

A sign of the more stormy waters the party was moving into came when John Gormley appointed Gerry McCaughey, the founder of Century Homes, the timber-frame housing company, as the new Chair of the Dublin Docklands Development Authority.

The Authority had become mired in controversies. The relationship between board membership of the Authority and the ongoing involvement of Anglo Irish Bank quite frankly stank. The bloated sale and purchase of the Irish Glass Bottle site in Ringsend was being investigated. As the Minister now responsible, Gormley wanted a presence on the board who would get to the root of these controversies.

Three weeks later, a news story broke stating that McCaughey had avoided tax through a legal mechanism that had existed then but was now closed. This allowed assets in a spouse's name to be transferred to another country, in this case Italy, reducing tax liability. He had not acted illegally, but the perception was that he could not now act credibly to clean up the Dublin Docklands Development Authority.

John Gormley acted quickly in requesting his resignation. The opposition had a field day, with Labour leader Eamon Gilmore calling McCaughey a 'Green crony' despite him previously having been an election candidate for the Progressive Democrats. John would regret having been pressured into making such a decision.

In another attempt to make an independent appointment to this position, John Gormley later appointed Professor Niamh Brennan, an acknowledged expert in business ethics as Chair of the DDDA. Professor Brennan was also the wife of John Gormley's long-time political opponent Michael McDowell.

In April, Déirdre de Búrca launched her campaign for the Dublin European Parliament seat at the Trinity College Science Gallery. The launch was being done by Eamon Ryan, and I was MC for the evening. In the middle of proceedings, a voice message was left on my phone. It was from the Department of Finance. The message was asking me to contact the Minister for Finance urgently. I stole away from the function and rang the Department.

Brian Lenihan told me that he had met with the board of Irish Nationwide Building Society that day. The board was agitated, he claimed, at my criticism of its long-time Chief Executive, Michael Fingleton. The criticisms centring on his acceptance of a €1m bonus payment, his accumulation of a massive personal pension fund, as well as his general management of what was meant to be a mutual building society were all matters of significant public concern.

The Minister was telling me that he was uncomfortable to be receiving such criticism. I was unsure why he was telling me. I felt that it reflected an unwillingness to take on the financial establishment, as well as a distance from public anger at the activities of those individuals and the institutions of which they were a part. As far as I was concerned, Michael Fingleton and the Irish Nationwide Building Society personified and represented much of what had come to be wrong within Irish financial services. I was shocked by the conversation, and by Lenihan's attitude. It did not change my perspective on Irish Nationwide or Mr Fingleton.

I never had much of that type of contact with Brian Lenihan. One other occasion on which he contacted me was in relation to approving the appointment of Colm O'Doherty to the top position in Allied Irish Bank. O'Doherty had been an AIB insider who was indelibly linked with the decisions that led it to where it was. A number of business correspondents had warned me that O'Doherty shouldn't be appointed. Brian Lenihan wanted to see him appointed, and was ringing me to sound me out as I had expressed public reservations. The appointment was made subject to a time-limited review, a change of title, roles and responsibilities. When O'Doherty resigned thirteen months later, I felt that it was clear that it had never been the right appointment.

We were in the middle of election campaigns, where local and European issues were meant to come to the fore, and yet the banking issue continued to dominate. In the local elections the Greens were defending 18 city and county council seats. There had been two high-profile defections from the party, and a third councillor was being replaced very close to the election. The hope remained that the party could retain its local government presence.

One of the difficulties that the Green Party had faced throughout its history was achieving electoral success in proper proportions. Greatest success was achieved in European elections, less so in Dáil elections, but still at a greater level than had ever been achieved through local elections. As a result, there was a lopsidedness to the type of representatives who were elected for the Green Party.

As a small party, the Greens had never achieved an effective local base. Not all local electoral areas were contested. The percentage of the national vote was never higher than 3.5%. Even so, up until April 2009 the hope of retaining Green local government seats seemed realistic. Opinion polls in

April showed the first fall in Green Party support since the party had entered into government. What had seemed to have happened was that the election campaign had begun properly and in earnest. Opposition party candidates were finding easy pickings on the doorsteps. Voters were all too willing to say that they going to vote against Fianna Fáil. A vote against the Greens was seen as being 'much the same thing', or so opposition canvassers suggested.

The need to introduce a supplementary budget in April as a response to the inadequate way in which the October 2008 budget was handled proved to be another nail in the coffin of whatever remaining respect the public might have had for the government.

The Green campaign was already cursed from its out-set. A printer had approached the party with a proposal for 'sustainable' election posters that involved the image being printed directly onto a wooden board. Most candidates followed this approach, which involved payment up front. When posters started being erected in May, high winds soon showed them to be totally unsuitable. Candidates were left with a collection of cracked and damaged posters with a printer unwilling to repay their money.

The largest number of posters were ordered by Déirdre de Búrca, which resulted in an enormous personal cost to her. The cost of her campaign would lead to much of the unhappiness Déirdre was to experience with the party. Several dozen local election candidates were simi-larly affected, if on a smaller scale. For people who had put themselves forward voluntarily, carrying most of their own expenses, this fiasco did a lot to undermine much-needed confidence in the campaign.

The reaction on the doorsteps was the worst that Green Party candidates had ever experienced. Real anger existed. Education issues were very much to the fore. If there was a sector of the population where it could be physically seen that the Green Party vote had been damaged, it was with women with young children in education. In a weak voting base, this had been an important part of the Green Party vote.

How we organised the campaign was not making it easier to achieve results either. For my Munster campaign, my near indifference allowed others to call all the shots. My poster image was far from warm. A severe haircut with once-worn wraparound glasses gave me appearance, rightly identified by Harry McGee of *The Irish Times*, of a German technocrat. While I had no hope of being elected in Munster, there was a slim chance that Déirdre de Búrca might win through in Dublin. The elephant in the room was the question of the intentions of Patricia McKenna. Patricia had not sought the party's nomination. She had been consistent in opposing the party entering government. The failure to get a two thirds majority to support the Lisbon Treaty gave Patricia the freedom to be actively involved in the 'No' campaign.

She never hid her unhappiness at the direction the party was taking, but neither did she seek to undermine. Still, with the European elections approaching, there was an expectation that she would not be standing by. And so it came to pass. Under the pretext of the government pushing forward with a second referendum on the Lisbon Treaty, Patricia McKenna declared her candidacy as an independent. With that announcement went any hope of winning a seat in Dublin.

The priority for the party became the local elections. As the last week of the campaigns began, the party leadership began to consider where the party would be after the elections, with the government approaching the likely mid-term point of its life. I was campaigning in Kerry, and I wanted to make a statement saying that the programme for government should be reviewed. My chosen means to communicate this intention was a tweet.

I had taken up social networking in February, having been persuaded to do so by Niamh FitzGibbon, a candidate for the party in New Ross. Having dabbled on Facebook, I soon discovered Twitter. I was taken by its informal, spontaneous nature. I saw its potential as an election tool. On Twitter I chose the handle 'sendboyle', as in 'Send Boyle to Brussels', and it was also a nice pun on being a Senator. Spontaneous as Twitter is, in this instance I told the Green parliamentary party of my intention to tweet and sought its agreement.

The tweet was picked up by the media. The reaction of the Taoiseach was dismissive, but that was part of a pattern that followed several of my interventions. On issues like the number of junior ministers, ministerial pay and others, the pattern was firstly dismissive comment from the Taoiseach's office, followed by eventual action on the issue raised.

It wasn't helped by the official line taken by the party, which regularly stressed that I was speaking in a personal capacity. I rarely was. I was Chair of the party, but often felt undermined with this lack of support. It caused unnecessary confusion with the media. Nevertheless, the interventions usually achieved their desired goal, as was the case with new negotiations on a reviewed programme for government, a process that began once the European and Local elections had finished. Other interventions on the number on junior ministers, on ministerial pay and political expenses were also successful.

My excursions into social media were to prove a double-edged sword. I was attracted by the level of engagement with people that didn't seem to exist in traditional media. People were attracted to my sites seeing me as a siphon through which to express their anger and frustration, sometimes quite viciously. It took me sometime to identify those who wanted responses from those who endlessly engaged in mud-slinging. Different people from different parts of the country who became a useful sounding board on what the country was going through. Some interacted with each other as well as with me. Some like Ciara Brown in Dublin, Nicola Coffey in Kerry and Gráinne Fallon in Offaly formed a Greek chorus on my Facebook page in their attempts to ensure I was aware of their ongoing worries.

A mid-term review of the programme of government was necessary, and was always likely. More cynical voices would have seen it as an attempt to deflect attention from what had been a fairly disastrous set of elections for the Greens, and it was true that we certainly didn't want to dwell on those results. We had fallen from eighteen city and county council seats to three. Surprisingly, the number of Green town council seats increased marginally from twelve to fifteen.

In the European elections, Déirdre de Búrca had a pyrrhic victory of sorts when she outpolled Patricia McKenna. However, she failed to clear the 5% threshold that would have allowed her to claim some of her election expenses back, adding to her growing unhappiness, and to her perception of not having been given adequate support from the party.

In Munster, I polled a not particularly impressive 3% of the vote, although that had been the highest vote won by a Green candidate in that constituency, which I didn't feel too bad about. In Northern Ireland, the Green candidate Stephen Agnew recorded a similar vote. Given that he was coming from a totally different base, we were very pleased with that result.

The European elections were an exercise in hope. It was in the local elections that the Green Party felt the most hurt. With those results, dissension within the party grew. While the circumstances surrounding the elections were less than ideal, and with a little less bad luck the overall result would not have been so bad, it remained an appalling result for the party. The return of city and county council seats was the lowest since the first contested set of local elections by the party in 1985.

The numbers of votes wasn't too far below what the party had received in the local elections of 2004. It was the same as had been won in 1999 with a better return. What had changed was that the Greens had ceased to be a 'transfer friendly' party, so the transfers needed to push candidates over the line for final seats in constituencies never materialised. There were some agonising near-victories, where a handful of votes would have changed the result. Closest was Joe Corr in Balbriggan, but also close was Niall O'Brolchain in Galway and Terence Corish in South Dublin. A half a dozen additional seats could have been won with a better bounce of the ball.

In the midst of this disaster, the party sought to gain some solace from the victories that had been achieved, hoping to learn some lessons. In retaining his seats on Kilkenny County Council and Borough Council, Malcolm Noonan actually managed to increase his vote.

Brian Meaney in Ennis in Clare managed the same feat. In Louth the party achieved its best success, with Mark Dearey graduating from Dundalk Town Council to Louth County Council. Mark also held on to his town council seat where he was joined by Marianne Butler, with Mary Kavanagh winning a first-time seat on Ardee Town Council. In Wexford, the party got first-time representation on Wexford Borough Council through Danny Forde after several near misses, and Niamh FitzGibbon followed in the footsteps of her Aunt and her Grandmother in being elected to New Ross Town Council.

Two by-elections were held on the same day as the local and European elections. The Dublin South by-election was caused by the death of Seamus Brennan in the previous July, and there was a vacancy in Dublin Central following the death of Tony Gregory in January. The Greens didn't contest Dublin Central, but Dublin South was the constituency of Eamon Ryan and an obligation to contest existed.

Elizabeth Davidson was selected as the Green candidate for Dublin South. Nervous and inexperienced, she didn't help her campaign when, on a candidates' debate on the Pat Kenny radio show, she claimed that natural gas was not a fossil fuel. Not that there was an expectation that a seat could be won. Once Fine Gael had persuaded George Lee, RTÉ's economics editor, to stand as their candidate, no other candidate was likely to succeed.

George Lee was elected with a phenomenal 54% of the vote. The victory of Maureen O'Sullivan, Tony Gregory's successor, in Dublin Central (where David Geary flew the flag for the Greens) showed that the anti-government vote was dispersing in many directions.

The election results had increased the pressure between the parties of government. In July, this manifested itself with a debate in the Seanad on the Criminal Justice (Amendment) Bill. The bill, in its main thrust dealing with gangland crime, was not particularly contentious. As the bill was progressing through the Dáil, the Greens had asked the Minister responsible to introduce an amendment for an annual review of the legislation to guard against civil liberties concerns. He said that the issue would be addressed in the Seanad.

When, during the Seanad debate, no mention was made of the change, and nor was any amendment forthcoming, along with Déirdre de Búrca we chose to visibly abstain from the bill.

There was, by this stage, considerable history between Dermot Ahern and the Greens. The list of Green grievances was growing. Beginning with his continuous foot-dragging on the Civil Partnership Bill, and continuing with unnecessarily bringing back blasphemy into the Defamation Bill, complicating the Immigration and Residency Bill, being utterly unhelpful on rendition flights through Shannon and what the Greens believed was an almost vendetta approach to equality issues, especially the Equality Authority.

Through the Summer, the *Sunday Tribune* had conducted a long-running campaign on the issue of political and particularly ministerial expenses, led by its journalist Ken Foxe. Each minister came under the microscope. Use of the government jet was a particular bugbear. The Green ministers had chosen not to use the jet. Eamon Ryan was on board two flights from Brussels that had been organised for other ministers. It was John Gormley, who didn't use the jet, who was more subject to the *Sunday Tribune's* finger wagging. Having decided to travel on an official visit to the UK, firstly by using a ferry to Wales, the Irish embassy in London organised car transport for the rest of the visit. Its cost was far in excess of the price of commercial flights to make the same visit.

The real victim of this campaign was the Ceann Comhairle John O'Donoghue. His expenses as Minister for Arts, Sports and Tourism made for uncomfortable reading.

When he was challenged by the leader of the Labour Party Eamon Gilmore, his position became untenable. O'Donoghue did approach John Gormley for support from the Greens. He had done an effective job as Ceann Comhairle, but his position was impossible. It wasn't a factor at the time, but it would have been difficult for the Greens to give a life-raft to the man responsible for the 'Greens are like a slug on lettuce' remark.

The Summer of 2009 seemed to be a series of overlapping scandals. Overspending in FÁS came to represent everything that had been wrong with governmental expenditure during the era of the Celtic Tiger. Its Chief Executive Rody Molloy seemed to symbolise the excesses of the organisation. He had to go. However, the manner of his leaving was to create more public anger. The Minister for Enterprise and Tánaiste Mary Coughlan agreed, in order to end his contract and move him on more quickly, to a retirement package for him far in excess of what he should have been entitled to. The lessons of Patrick Neary in leaving the Financial Regulator's office had not been learned. Once again, someone was being seen to be rewarded for not having done their job properly.

The difference this time was that it wasn't a standalone board making this decision, but a government minister, albeit one who had not consulted the Cabinet. The advice being given to the Cabinet by the Attorney General was that these packages could not be challenged. According to him, there existed a concept of 'legitimate expectation', where what had been given cannot be easily taken away. I argued with John and Eamon and Donal Geoghegan that each of these packages should be challenged. Even if successful court actions were taken, it would be better than being supine and creating ever more public anger.

The fallout from the various elections was creating vacancies elsewhere. The election of Alan Kelly as a Labour MEP for Munster created a Seanad vacancy that necessitated a by-election, a rare enough political occurrence. There were now two vacancies, as Fianna Fáil Senator (and Bertie Ahern ally) Tony Kett had sadly passed away. This eventuality hadn't been covered by the programme for government agreement. There was an assumption within Fianna Fáil that it would fill all vacancies. It was an assumption that I questioned. I secured an agreement with Donie Cassidy, Fianna Fáil's leader in the Seanad, that the two parties should rotate contesting Seanad vacancies. Approving this agreement, John Gormley got Brian Cowen as Taoiseach to agree that the Greens would contest the first vacancy.

With the government majority in both Houses of the Oireachtas, the prospect of a third Green Senator became real. This meant that the party had to have an internal selection process, involving all the elected Green Party representatives. The party leadership would have preferred it if the next most successful candidate from the 2007 general election were selected. This would have been Mark Dearey from Louth.

Other names were talked about. Tendai Mandondo, a Zimbabwean immigrant, had been a strong candidate for the party in the local elections. Her selection would have been a powerful statement. Unfortunately, she had yet to receive Irish citizenship.

The uber-democracy within the party meant that this was a vacancy that any member of the party could seek to contest. Niall O'Brolchain, former Mayor of Galway, wanted to be considered. For the past number of years Niall had been the parliamentary group secretary for the party, and had also worked as liaison for our local government representatives, as well as having a development role within the party.

These roles gave Niall a natural advantage in knowing how the party worked, and how best to persuade those who would be making this decision. It was an advantage he used skilfully, narrowly edging out Mark Dearey for the party's nomination. After besting the internal machinations of the Green Party, winning a Seanad by-election proved far easier, and the Green Party had its third Senator.

Niall's role within the party was taken up by Loretta Ristic, who became membership organiser – a role she was to play enthusiastically under the most difficult of circumstances.

Before the Seanad by-elections, and before negotiations on a review of the programme for government, the government had the more pressing matter of a second referendum on the Lisbon Treaty to attend to. On July 7th, the party held another convention to determine its position on the second holding of a referendum on the Lisbon Treaty. Opinion in the party had remained static. When a vote was taken, the result was 214 votes to 107, exactly the two-thirds majority needed to allow the party to campaign for the Treaty. One of our newly elected local government representatives later told me that, having voted against in the initial vote, she subsequently abstained for the second, a decision that was to make a crucial difference.

In October, the voters in the country reconsidered the Lisbon Treaty, and there was a massive reversal in votes. The change of heart may have been driven partly by the more animated campaigns run by political parties, but more likely was a result of growing economic fears and the feeling that those could best be addressed in a European context.

As with the Nice Treaty, the re-holding of a referendum caused controversy. I've always found this to be a hollow argument. Referenda on the same subject can be, and should be, held regularly. It remains the sovereign right of the people to say no. In changed circumstances, there is nothing improper about asking the people once again.

One of the sadder casualties during the Greens' period in government was the resignation, on the issue of a second Lisbon referendum, of the party's head of research, Carol Fox, whose workload transferred to Kerrie O'Brien. Carol had had a long-time association with the party, being especially close to John Gormley, having been his director of elections on a number of occasions. Carol's background with CND and the Peace and Neutrality Alliance meant that she couldn't stand over a growing common foreign and security policy approach by Ireland in the European Union. Of all the resignations from the party, that was the most difficult. Unlike other departures, personal relations remained good. This wasn't about long-standing enmity or issues of ego or personal advancement. Carol's role was valued and would be missed.

With local elections, European elections, by-elections and now a referendum out of the way, negotiations began on a renewed programme for government. Several changes had occurred since the negotiations on the original programme. Bertie Ahern was no longer Taoiseach; Brian Cowen now was. Seamus Brennan had passed away, which meant that Noel Dempsey was the only original negotiator on the Fianna Fáil side. On this occasion he was joined by Mary Hanafin as Minister for Social Protection, and Dermot Ahern as the Minister for Justice, seen by many in the Green Party as something of a *bête noire*.

There were changes of necessity too in the Green Party negotiating team. John Gormley was now party leader. Donal Geoghegan was operating as programme manager in the Department of the Taoiseach, in effect a civil servant.

I was the only remaining Green negotiator from 2007. In their places, John appointed Eamon Ryan and our Deputy Leader Mary White.

A difficulty in the composition of our negotiating team was the question of who would be leader of the delegation. As Party Chair, and as the most experienced negotiator for the party, I felt that I should fill that role. Eamon felt that as a Cabinet Minister he would be diminished in negotiating with his 'peers' if he wasn't in that role. John Gormley's decision was to make no decision. We went in to the talks with no person appointed. It wasn't helpful.

I sat in the central chair. Eamon made an opening statement. I dealt with the issues as they arose; Eamon dealt with the wider media. We had fallen into the old Green habit of everyone being the leader and no one being the leader. But there were more serious problems than that. Mary White and I worried that far too often Eamon approached issues from the perspective of a Cabinet meeting rather than that of the Green Party. At times it seemed like there were four negotiators against two.

The Greens' position had already been undermined by the publication of an internal strategy discussion document that had been released to the media on the second day of the talks. It was an earlier draft of the document, which meant that its source had to be a member the Green parliamentary party. It wasn't leaked by the party leader, nor was it any member of the negotiating team. That limited the number of people it could have been, but no one was identified. Suspicions existed that weren't pursued. Whoever it was thought they were being helpful. They weren't.

Despite those obstacles, the advantage in these negotiations was with the Green Party. Fianna Fáil's strategy seemed to be to exaggerate particular areas of Green demands to head off those policy areas that were more important to the party. In their media briefings and in the negotiations, obsessive interest was placed by the Fianna Fáil team on the Green Party position on animal welfare. This was important to the Greens, but nowhere near as important as was being made out.

On one day of the talks, out of what seemed nothing, Mary Hanafin went on something of a rant. 'All you seem to care about are hares, stags and badgers,' she charged. Later it was learned, after the WikiLeaks revelations in 2011, that she went from that day's negotiations to repeat that accusation at a reception at the American Embassy. What she didn't report was Mary White's riposte to her: 'And all you care about are builders, bankers and bailouts.'

The Greens' real priority was Education. The party's internal discussions were hugely influenced by Paul Gogarty, who had been a very effective Chair of the Oireachtas Committee on Education, and had raised education issues to be red-line issues for the party in these negotiations. On issues such as maintaining the primary pupil-teacher ratio, protecting school grants and ensuring that there would be no reintroduction of third-level fees, Greens felt that protecting education had an important economic as well as a social purpose.

What was agreed in Education hadn't been enough for Paul Gogarty. He didn't consider that the effort he had put in was worth what had been agreed. Through the intervention of Senator Joe O'Toole, the general secretaries of each of the Teachers unions were contacted. They stated that they were satisfied with what the Greens had achieved. This seemed to satisfy Paul. His obstinacy had achieved some effect, but many of us in the parliamentary party were annoyed by his tactics, such as his temporary resignation as party Education Spokesperson.

Political reform was next highest on the Green agenda. Ending corporate donations, changing the structure of government through local government reforms and the introduction of regional government, and a hatful of constitutional reforms were the opportunities that the Greens believed needed to be grasped. Reform of politics, as far the Greens were concerned, had to be the antidote to a difficult economic situation.

The overriding concern, though, was the economic situation. The spin against the Greens was that the programme was being reviewed without proper consideration of the economic reality. The opposite was the truth. Almost every new proposal or innovation in the document seeking to bring about economic stimulation came from the Greens. The position of the Fianna Fáil negotiators was passive, seeking to prevent change wherever possible. Outside of a proposal to move the Abbey Theatre to the GPO site on O'Connell Street in Dublin, it is hard to identify any proposal during these talks that came exclusively from Fianna Fáil.

One of our goals was to include an overhaul of taxation in the new programme, which was something that we felt was an important part of stimulating the economy. The Commission on Taxation, a vital plank of the original programme for government, had reported in September after eighteen months of deliberations. Its findings concurred with many of the changes that the Green Party had long been advocating. It was our belief that the Irish system of taxation had to be made more diverse, that the reliance on large, one-off taxes was unsustainable and had to be replaced with more varied taxes. We also believed that all the unfair tax reliefs, which had created so many problems, had to go. Of course, there is no political advantage in trying to bring about real tax reform; it enabled others to be por- tray the Greens as a tax-more party, rather than a tax-fairer and tax-more-effectively party.

Nevertheless, progress was being made. We were shap- ing a programme for government, even with the economic constraints under which we were operating, that we would have wanted to have agreed in 2007. The biggest lesson that had been learned between 2007 and 2009 was in having control of the script. For the revision of the programme of government, the Greens had control of the script. As a result, the contents of the agreement better reflected Green Party thinking.

Even so, it could have been better. The final drafting, which in 2007 had taken place between me and Noel Dempsey, would now take place between Dempsey and Eamon Ryan. Suffering from a bad cold I had stood aside, believing that most of the agreement had been reached. During the draft- ing process important areas of agreement were put aside, probably in the interests of Cabinet collegiality.

Not appearing in the final draft was an agreement to implement the Stockholm Convention, the application of which would have made the introduction of incineration even more difficult. A more serious omission was a hard- won concession from Dermot Ahern that a referendum be held to remove the reference to blasphemy from the con- stitution. The passing of Defamation Act earlier in 2009, at the insistence of Dermot Ahern and the Attorney General, recodifying the crime of blasphemy, was one of the more embarrassing tasks that the Green Party members of the Oireachtas had to undertake.

Despite this, the agreement contained much of which Green Party members could be proud. The difficulty was that approval of the new programme of government by the Green Party membership would be linked to the end of the consultation process on NAMA and another party decision on whether Green members of the Oireachtas should also support this initiative.

Not that it was it was an either/or situation. Failure to approve to the Programme for Government would mean having to leave government. Failure to approve NAMA would mean the same. On October 10th, the latest in a series of Green Party Special Members' conventions was organised for the library at the RDS in Ballsbridge, in antici-pation of the largest attendance at such a meeting since the party had decided to enter into government at the Mansion House in June 2007.

The pre-meeting spin varied, from us being a party now dominated by new members to us being a party whose deci-sions were being made by members whose only issue of concern was that of animal welfare. Neither was true. Green Party members whose membership is six months duration or less are not allowed to vote at Green Party conventions. The over-hyping of the animal welfare issue that began within the negotiations, continued with this special convention and would continue to be hyped in the following months was in reality true of no more than two-dozen people who had animal welfare as their sole concern that day.

The grouping opposed to NAMA under any circum-stances tabled a number of procedural amendments for the RDS meeting. As Party Chair, and chair of the meeting for the day, I allowed the meeting to open discussion of these amendments. After ten minutes of debate it was clear to me, and many others in the hall, that the purpose of these amendments was to frustrate debate. I put an immediate motion to the floor on whether the members wanted to approve the agenda that had been decided by the party's National Council. The meeting overwhelmingly approved the proposed agenda, allowing me as chair to guillotine the procedural amendments.

The meeting had been organised by having debates and making decisions on the reviewed programme for government ahead of the debate on NAMA. The hope was that the changes achieved in the new programme for government would create a momentum for a 'Yes' vote.

However, the day did not continue smoothly. The shortened debate of procedural issues had to be followed immediately with a recess, as copies of the new programme for government had yet to be printed. Conspiracy theorists believed this to be an attempt to avoid people giving it proper scrutiny. It just wasn't ready in time.

It took 30 minutes for the meeting to recommence. There followed a series of passionate speeches. It was clear that the programme itself would be approved. What wasn't so clear was whether the vote on NAMA could pass. More confusion was caused when the time allocated for the first motion ate into the time allocated for the second. Ballot boxes for both motions had to be opened simultaneously while the second motion was being debated. It was a decision made to facilitate those members from outside Dublin depending on public transport.

Other confusion was caused through the wording of the second motion, with many present unable to understand whether it was worded negatively or positively. This worried John Gormley, who in the voting room made an impromptu speech asking members to be sure they were aware of what they were voting for.

When the votes were collated, I had the responsibility as Party Chair to make the public announcement. As the announcement was being broadcast on tv and radio I decided to make the announcement as gaeilge, in my very poor Irish. The assembled media initially misunderstood, and began scribbling excitedly at the prospect of the government falling. In whatever language, the results were quite emphatic. The new programme for government was approved by the same proportion of members that approved the decision to enter into government: 84%. The vote on NAMA was less emphatic, but still significant at 69% approval.

The recourse of the Green Party to total party democracy was not being received well elsewhere. It added to the sense of agitation that some people had with the Greens that such a small group should have such an influence on the life of the nation.

The party had decided to continue in government. There would still be the question of another austerity budget to be introduced by the end of the year, as well as Paul Gogarty having a star turn. As the year ended, the only consolation that seemed to exist was that 2010 couldn't be any worse.

10 | Resigned to Fate

Budget 2010 was the third budget in 14 months that sought to reduce the deficit as well as government expenditure. This budget wanted to achieve an adjustment of €4 billion, the largest adjustment to date. It seemed unremitting in its misery.

It was the first budget that the Green party supported where basic social welfare payments were under threat. The Greens were proposing a 3-year freeze. While the budget would increase with the sadly additional numbers on the unemployment register, it was in our opinion the best means of keeping the largest area of government expenditure under control. The Department of Finance were arguing for a 6% decrease across the board. Fianna Fáil was insisting, based on their knowledge that older people were more inclined to vote, and more inclined to vote for them, that the State pension remain untouched. In what was now a deflationary environment, we argued that at the very least any decrease in social welfare payments should not be any greater than the decrease in the cost of living, so that the real value of payments could be maintained.

Fianna Fáil got its way to relation to leaving the State pension untouched. Social welfare payments, including disability and carers' payments, were reduced by 4.1%. It was the most unpopular decision this government made; a decision from which it was impossible to recover.

In the aftermath of the programme for government renegotiations, The Greens exercised whatever influence we had to mitigate the effects of this budget. Some areas of expenditure were increased, such as investment in improving water services. The funds available for energy efficiency and warmer homes schemes were increased. Some expenditure areas were protected, such as important parts of the education budget. John Gormley succeeded in having the homelessness section of his department's budget maintained.

Other areas of expenditure had their budgets cut to a lesser degree than others. The arts budget, overseas development aid and youth services were areas that were protected. We viewed these areas as important, but also realised that there was no political benefit in doing what we believed to be the right thing.

Carbon Tax was introduced. As necessary as this was to avoid future reliance on unsustainable taxes like stamp duty and VAT on house sales, it was also clear that it was seen as a political negative. The introduction of a €200 charge on second homes was seen as more socially progressive. To mitigate the introduction of a Carbon Tax, we secured an increase in the fuel allowance; again, something for which no political credit would be forthcoming.

Another positive, and a long-lasting positive, that came from Budget 2009 was the introduction of the 'Bike to Work' tax relief. It was a tax relief of which we could be proud: at a relatively low cost, it was later credited with putting 40,000 people back on bikes.

The compromise came in accepting a car scrappage scheme. This was nothing more than the usual catering to the pleading of special interest groups that had so bedevilled the taxation system. There was no reason why the motor industry should have been given this exemption. As an industry that imports into the country it has a negative effect on the balance of payments, and now was to be further subsidised. At least the Greens managed to mitigate its worst effects by having the scheme only apply to smaller, more environmentally friendly cars. A more generous incentive towards the purchase of electric vehicles was meant to push new car buyers in a different direction.

These positives didn't go anywhere near assuaging continuing public anger with a series of austerity budgets. This anger was being especially felt by Green Party staff. The tirade of sometimes quite vicious phone calls, texts, letters, emails and social network messages were of a volume and intensity that went beyond what was reasonable or forgivable. As bad a reaction as many of the Green Oireachtas members were receiving, it was worse being shielded by an all-too-loyal staff who took more abuse than any person should. In our head office in Suffolk Street, Ed Davitt was the person who shouldered much of this abuse. I realised far too late the level of vitriol my constituency secretary, Edel Boyce, had to put up with. The same was true throughout the Green Party organisation.

The pressure began to manifest itself in the strangest of ways. During the budget debate in the Dail, goaded by the Labour Party's Emmet Stagg, Paul Gogarty snapped. Pausing briefly to apologise for what he was about to utter, he went on to say: 'Fuck you, Deputy Stagg! Fuck you!' The clip of this outburst would go on to become an enormous YouTube hit.

John Gormley had always given a lot of latitude to Paul Gogarty. Many in the Green parliamentary party were often exasperated with his unpredictability and his perceived lack of patience. There was also an understanding of the personal problems that Paul had been living through. His father Billy, then the serving Mayor of South Dublin County Council, passed away in 2008. This happened a short number of years after Paul's trusted friend and confidant Fintan McCarthy had died in a tragic accident in China. There were times when members of the Green parliamentary party admired Paul's single-mindedness. There can be no doubting the committed campaign that Paul ran within the party to make education the priority issue in advance of the negotiations on the review of the programme for government. His outburst provoked a mixture of embarrassment and envy. It was known that a level of provocation existed. Many of us would have liked to allow ourselves to speak so honestly.

The Budget coincided with an important international event in which Greens throughout the world had invested a great deal of hope. The framework conference on climate change was meeting in Copenhagen. This was intended to build on the Kyoto Protocol, which was due to be replaced in 2012. That conference turned out to be a huge disappointment, nevertheless Irish Greens took some pride in the fact that the only Green Minister for the Environment who attended the conference was John Gormley.

After the budget debate, the Dáil and the Seanad rose for the Christmas recess. December had only a few days remaining when the most stunning political news of the year was revealed, and not in the most satisfactory way either. TV3 News reported that the Minister for Finance Brian Lenihan had been diagnosed as having pancreatic cancer. Everyone in Irish political life was stunned by this news. There was continual political disagreement about decisions that were and had to be taken in government, but there was a good working relationship between Brian Lenihan and the Greens. Eamon Ryan had developed an especially close relationship. The news dominated political discussions as 2010 began.

Meanwhile, after his spectacular by-election victory, George Lee seemed to cut a rather forlorn figure in Leinster House. Fine Gael didn't seem to know what to do with him. They had sent him on a successful nationwide tour feeding off government unpopularity. Back in the Dáil chamber his presence seemed superfluous. Neither was he given the commitments that he wanted as to what role he would play in a post-election situation. With a deadline approaching on whether his job in RTÉ would be kept open, he decided to end his 9-month flirtation with politics. Lee announced his resignation at the beginning of February. His would be but the first in a series of political skittles that would fall over in the incredible few weeks to follow.

Between the agreement of a new programme for government and the making of the budget statement, there was a little matter of selecting an Irish nominee for the new European Commission. There were several months of speculation prior to the making of the appointment. While a number of Fianna Fáil ministers wanted to be considered for the position, the political arithmetic of the Dáil made this impossible. The media had raised the prospect of Pat Cox becoming a Commissioner. While there would be wide political divergences between Pat Cox and the Greens, both John Gormley and Eamon Ryan would have been prepared to accept his nomination, based on his wide-ranging European experience.

Taoiseach Brian Cowen informed the Cabinet that he had been asked by the Commission's President José Manuel Barroso to ensure that Ireland nominate a woman to help the new Commission achieve a better gender balance. Brian Cowen wanted to nominate Máire Geoghegan-Quinn, then serving a second term as the Irish nominee at the Court of Auditors in Luxembourg. The Green Party was not enthusiastic about Máire Geoghegan-Quinn being appointed as a Commissioner, believing that other candidates were more suitable and better qualified. The Green Party did not seek the post, though, and took the position that ultimately it was it was for the Taoiseach to call.

The Greens did believe that there should be a Green influence in the Cabinet of whoever was to be appointed as Commissioner. Déirdre de Búrca argued this most strongly within the Green parliamentary party, and wanted to play this role. John Gormley was happy to propose her, knowing that Déirdre had now given up on the idea of contesting future elections. He informed Brian Cowen that Green support for Máire Geoghegan-Quinn was contingent on such a position being made available. The Taoiseach came back to John Gormley to say that he was agreeable to that, and that Máire Geoghegan-Quinn was agreeable as well.

The appointment was made at the end of November. A Cabinet wouldn't be formed until after a European Parliament ratification process in January. Informal contact was made between Déirdre de Búrca and Máire Geoghegan-Quinn. The conversation was terse, and no mention was made about a Cabinet position. After Geoghegan-Quinn had been ratified, Déirdre de Búrca was becoming more nervous with each passing week about whether this change would happen or not. It turned out that Máire Geoghegan-Quinn did not feel obligated to honour this agreement. She had in fact reneged.

Déirdre learned of her not being appointed on meeting Mary Harney in a Leinster House corridor. That she hadn't learned from a Green Party source greatly added to her sense of grievance and agitation. She struck out wildly at those she believed were responsible: John Gormley and the Greens' programme manager Donal Geoghegan. She cut off all contact with the Green parliamentary party. As the person closest to her in the parliamentary party, I felt this most strongly, as did Eamon Ryan, her longest known friend in the party. Déirdre was the Godmother of one of his children.

Despite holding him partially responsible, Deirdre would only speak to Donal Geoghegan, cutting off communication from all members of the parliamentary party. She became increasingly strident in her demands. An alternative position was offered in the Cabinet of the Irish nominee to the Court of Auditors. As it was based in Luxembourg and not Brussels, it was not thought suitable.

Over the previous few months there had been media speculation that I would be offered the vacancy in the Court of Auditors. It was thought that the rumour was coming from the Taoiseach's office, on the basis that Luxembourg was a safer place for me to be.

I have to admit to having been intrigued, and more than a little interested, on becoming aware of those reports. I asked John Gormley to ask the Taoiseach whether there was any foundation to these reports. The Taoiseach indicated that he wasn't responsible for the speculation. In any case, John Gormley indicated that he wanted me to stay in Dublin, and so the party's efforts went towards securing a European position for Déirdre de Búrca.

As Déirdre's self-imposed deadline approached, Eamon Ryan made one last-ditch attempt to talk to her at her home. She refused to talk to him. On February 11th, Deirdre announced her resignation from Seanad Éireann. Coming little more than a week after the resignation of George Lee, with the main opposition party on the back foot, it was hardly ideal timing.

That Sunday, on Valentine's Day, while visiting the National Gallery with a very good friend of mine, I was asked to do an interview on the *This Week* programme on RTÉ Radio 1. I found an alcove in which to speak while my friend waited. It was one of the most difficult interviews I have ever done; trying to be fair to my closest colleague while presenting the best case for the party being, and remaining, in government.

Two high-profile political resignations over such a short period of time would have usually sustained the political rumour mill for the rest of the year, but within a short few weeks that would prove to have been only the halfway point.

In Limerick, an aside from Minister for Defence Willie O'Dea made during the white heat of the local election campaign was creating legal as well as political fallout. A comment made by O'Dea to a local reporter suggested that Sinn Féin candidate Maurice Quinlivan should be concerned with a family connection to an alleged brothel in the city. Legal proceedings followed, with an affidavit provided by O'Dea not being seen to be consistent with a subsequent statement.

Fine Gael Senator Eugene Regan began following this issue doggedly, claiming that the veracity of a Cabinet Minister was an issue of public confidence. Fine Gael chose to take the issue to the Dáil floor. Its announcement of its intention to table the motion brought the usual government knee-jerk response of immediately tabling of a motion of confidence by the Government Chief Whip, Pat Carey.

When organising government business that morning, Pat Carey firstly told John Gormley, then told Donal Geoghegan, and finally told Ciarán Cuffe as Green Party Whip. No objections were raised. Later that day, in the coffee dock of Leinster House, I met with Donal Geoghegan and Ciarán Cuffe who told me about the vote of confidence, and that it would be supported by the party's TDs. I was furious. I wanted to know how the decision was made without a parliamentary party meeting being held.

Throughout the day I had received messages from Green Party members across the country stating their unhappiness at voting confidence in Willie O'Dea. Unhappy as I also was, I felt that there was little I could do about it.

John Gormley had not objected to a vote of confidence being taken, but he was not going to go on record as expressing confidence. Pat Carey wanted a Green speaker, a Green ministerial speaker. John would not participate in the debate, and insisted that Eamon Ryan speak instead. Eamon was reluctant. He later delivered a caveat-filled, equivocating speech that he was to later accept as his worst moment in politics:

> *Minister for Communications, Energy and Natural Resources (Deputy Eamon Ryan): I am speaking on behalf of the Green Party to set out how we see the issue. The Minister for Defence, Deputy O'Dea, has spoken to our party and set out his version of events...*
>
> *Deputy Pádraic McCormack: Is the Green Party happy with it?*
>
> *Deputy Eamon Ryan:... and we followed, with everyone else...*
>
> *Deputy Dinny McGinley: Which version?*
>
> *Deputy Eamon Ryan:... the various events as reported.*
>
> *Deputy Paul Connaughton: Is that why Senator de Búrca left?*
>
> *Deputy Eamon Ryan: It can be only on the basis of what one sees there that one makes a judgment and assessment. The facts are clear. They have been gone through, and I am sure they will be gone through further. Those*

facts are the original interview in the Limerick Chronicle following allegations of improper use of civil servants for political work; the allegations during the course of the interview regarding the use of the property by the people in question; the fact that the journalist then contacted those people...

Deputy Damien English: The Minister has lost his confidence.

Deputy Eamon Ryan: ... and asked for comment, and they threatened legal action against the newspaper, which led to publication of a clarification by the newspaper and the seeking of a High Court injunction against the Minister, Deputy Willie O'Dea, seeking that he would stop spreading allegations, as I see it...

Deputy Pádraic McCormack: Which side is the Minister on?

Deputy Eamon Ryan: In April last year the High Court refused an injunction on the basis of a strong denial by the Minister, Deputy O'Dea, that he was spreading allegations, and in June 2009 the person in question was elected to Limerick City Council and pursued a defamation action against the Minister, Deputy O'Dea, who filed an affidavit repeating his denial.

Deputy Ulick Burke: A lapse.

Deputy Eamon Ryan: This led to the discovery of a tape of the interview, which showed that the Minister had made such allegations. The crucial matter, as I understand it...

Deputy Michael Creed: The Minister's understanding is not great.

Deputy Eamon Ryan: ... is that at that point the Minister acknowledged that he had mistakenly stated he had not made the allegations...

Deputy Michael Creed: When he got caught.

Deputy Pádraic McCormack: Why would he do that?

Deputy Eamon Ryan: ... and that he had relied in making such an affidavit on the published interview and in December 2009...

(Interruptions).

Deputy Michael Creed: Get your gun now, Willie.

An Ceann Comhairle: Allow the Minister to continue without interruption.

Deputy Eamon Ryan: ... a High Court judge ruled that the case was settled with damages and costs paid by Deputy O'Dea to the person in question. The Minister, Deputy O'Dea, also withdrew and apologised for the wrongful allegations...

Deputy Pádraic McCormack: Do you think that is all right?

Deputy Eamon Ryan: ...which apology, as I understand, was accepted by the other party...

Deputy Simon Coveney: It is not about the other party.

Deputy Eamon Ryan: ... who also accepted that the earlier affidavit had been a mistake...

Deputy Joan Burton: Fianna Fáil is laughing at you.

(Interruptions).

Deputy Eamon Ryan: ... and was not an attempt to mislead. That is the crucial issue: when there was a mistake in the affidavit and something that was not true, it was acknowledged in court, dealt with in court, accepted by the other party and reported in the media as such. It was quite some time ago and I do not have the exact details.

Deputy Pádraic McCormack: What would you say if you were in opposition?

Deputy Eamon Ryan: As I see it that is the case...

Deputy Damien English: Sit down.

Deputy Eamon Ryan: ... and the circumstances have been set out and I do not hear any disagreement.

Deputy Paul Connaughton: You are uncomfortable and squirming.

Deputy Ulick Burke: They are bringing you down to their level.

Deputy Eamon Ryan: In those circumstances, our job in Government is to get on with the crucial issues that face this country and to start providing the jobs that were mentioned earlier on. That is the crucial task that we have in Government.

(Interruptions).

Deputy Eamon Ryan: I am happy that is what we should be concentrating on, confident that the Government can and will deliver on those jobs having delivered on the change to our budget and banking system, which will also help provide an economic turnaround.

Deputy Paul Connaughton: What a day for the Green Party.

Deputy Pádraic McCormack: The Green Party will save one job anyway ... Willie's.

Deputy Eamon Ryan: That is what the public is looking for us to do. That is what we intend to do in Government and will continue to do for the betterment of the country.

I watched the debate on the monitor in my office. With me was Ruth McLaughlin, an excellent intern from the Dublin City University graduate programme. I watched with disgust as Willie O'Dea and Dermot Ahern engaged in pantomime barracking of the opposition avoiding the central issue of confidence. I decided then that I would express my individual unhappiness. The issue of perjury was something the judicial system would determine; for me the real issue was the appropriateness of a Government minister talking about brothels and engaging in innuendo as a means of standard political discourse.

My first foray on the issue was responding to criticisms being made on Facebook. There I stated that I would not have voted confidence and believed that Willie O'Dea should resign. I later tweeted. I was fully conscious of what I was doing and the likely effect it would have, or if it didn't that I would have to resign.

Journalist followers picked up on what I was saying, realised its import and ran the story. By the following morning, what the Government had hoped was put to bed had extra legs. The Green parliamentary party met early that morning and stayed in session throughout the day. Ciarán Cuffe and Mary White expressed their disappointment that I had done what I done. Paul Gogarty had gone on the Morning Ireland programme to directly contradict me, saying that what Willie O'Dea did was wrong but that he shouldn't resign.

John Gormley and Eamon Ryan were not critical. I suspect that was because they realised that a mistake had been made in supporting the vote of confidence and it needed to be corrected. John spoke with Willie O'Dea, who told him that he would be exonerated by an article in the *Limerick Leader* due for publication on the following day.

Willie O'Dea was also to be interviewed on the *News at One* programme on RTÉ Radio 1. The interviewer Sean O'Rourke cut straight to the chase. 'Minister, you're a dirty little fighter, aren't you?' was his opening question. From then on in, O'Dea was on the defensive. The performance did nothing to inspire confidence.

Throughout the afternoon, John Gormley shuttled between the Taoiseach's office and the Green parliamentary meeting. It was clear that the Taoiseach didn't want and wasn't going to ask Willie O'Dea to resign. Late in the afternoon we received the proofs of the *Limerick Leader*. The article did not exonerate O'Dea.

By that stage, the vast majority of the Green parliamentary party believed that O'Dea had to go. We indicated that we were to issue a statement at six o'clock. That was taken as a signal by Fianna Fáil. Before six we were told that the Taoiseach was meeting Willie O'Dea. We held off making a statement until the results were known. Within the hour we were told that Willie O'Dea had resigned as Minister for Defence.

Whatever the politics of this controversy, it was clear that for most of the people involved we were now dealing with a whole new set of circumstances. On the following morning, Brian Cowen took John Gormley aside and asked plainly: 'John, what is this Twitter all about?'

For Assistant Government Press Secretary John Downing it caused more than a few problems. While John felt it part of his job to dampen down some of my outpourings, we had a good, strong relationship. There were times when I could have made life easier for him, but he accepted that there were times when I had to cut loose. In his jaded journalistic philosophy he would say: 'Dan, there are times you have to throw a few fucks into them.'

It was known that this episode would cause problems for the relations between the two parties of government. It was hoped that after this series of political resignations things would soon settle again. But we weren't finished yet.

Five days later, it was learned that the *Evening Herald* was to run a front page story on how Trevor Sargent was reputed to have interfered in a garda investigation. This was undoubtedly serious. Trevor had made an intervention, although the facts were nowhere near as straightforward as they were being portrayed. The constituent for whom Trevor had been making representations had undoubtedly been a victim in this process. There was also a concern that this story had come from a garda source.

In perception terms, Trevor knew that this could not be seen as positive. He resolved that he had to resign. His grace in accepting his position and acting quickly was a mark of his character. He had acted so speedily that the opposition parties had not had the opportunity to call for his resignation; instead they turned their fire on Fianna Fáil, suggesting that there was an element of payback over the Willie O'Dea affair.

I admit that I too had these suspicions, thinking that the Minister for Justice Dermot Ahern may have been involved. I soon came to be disabused of these notions, realising that the most likely source was a rogue element within the North Dublin Gardaí.

I was beginning to regret my initial tweet for unleashing this set of consequences. Someone, I felt, was motivated to point a finger at the Greens and suggest some kind of equivalence. The party was hurting as an honourable man was forced once again to stand aside.

It was meant to be a happy day for the Green Party. We had acted quickly to fill the vacancy caused by Déirdre de Búrca's resignation. The Taoiseach had appointed Mark Dearey to become the new Senator. That day was the day he was to be introduced to the Seanad. It was thought that maybe this could/should have been postponed, but too much organisation had occurred, and the party needed to show that it was willing to put its best foot forward.

11 | The Beginning of The End

The resignation merry-go-round had one more spin. In early March 2010, Martin Cullen, whose presence had been very subdued in recent months, announced that he would be resigning his position as Minister, citing ill health as the reason.

The announcement was greeted a bit mutedly. It was a resignation that helped in terms of Cabinet cohesion. Cullen had been a negative presence in the Cabinet for the Greens, reacting badly to many initiatives from Green ministers. As a previous Minister for the Environment, he was less than supportive on changing policy on incineration. He was most sullen at the decision by John Gormley to scrap electronic voting machines. It was a rare, popular decision. It was only political vanity keeping electronic voting machines in limbo. In the opinion of the Greens then, Cullen's departure was nothing to get upset about.

The political atmosphere matched the arctic conditions that Ireland was experiencing. It was the coldest winter in living memory. Ice was making many roads impassable, and walking on footpaths was nearly as difficult. The Cabinet National Emergency sub-committee was called into being. John Gormley, as Minister for the Environment, was given a co-ordinating role on this sub-committee. It was a role he took on reluctantly. He remembered as a young man the then Labour Party leader Michael O'Leary being dubbed the 'Minister for Snow' for being pushed forward in response to the weather emergency of 1981.

John felt as if he was being set up to take the obvious backlash that would arise from what could only be an extremely inadequate reaction to the crisis, especially from local authorities. His sense of being put upon was increased when he learned that the Minister for Transport Noel Dempsey was meant to share this responsibility, but was out of the country on a family holiday.

Although the conditions were worse than could reasonably have been anticipated, local authorities seemed particularly ill-prepared, with salt supplies soon running out. Roads became dangerous and closed off. John Gormley did traverse the country responding to the more damaged, isolated locations, however he resented that he seemed to carry this out on his own, with the Minister responsible for roads not in the country.

Government seemed to become a life of never ending crisis management. Early 2010, Donal Geoghegan came to a Green parliamentary party seeking a position on an issue that was exercising the Cabinet. The Attorney General wanted Ireland to be joined in a European Court action initiated by Italy in which Malta was also a co-respondent. The action centred around the right to display crucifixes in state schools.

We were astounded. Apparently this issue took up an hour and a half of the Cabinet's time. With the precarious condition of the Irish economy, that any time at all was being given to this issue, never mind the political fallout that would follow, showed a government with a tenuous hold on reality. The Greens made it quite clear that we could not support this measure.

As Taoiseach, Brian Cowen took his time about reshuffling the Cabinet. The first issue that had to be cleared up was the expectation that the Green Party had of a second Minister for State. The side (political) agreement between Bertie Ahern and Trevor Sargent in 2007 signed off on an additional Green Minister for State during any reshuffle that would happen around the anticipated halfway mark in the lifetime of the government.

This was intended to bring the Green Party up to the level of representation that smaller parties, like the Progressive Democrats and Democratic Left, had commanded in previous coalition governments. The danger was that publicly it would be seen as an exercise in political jobbery. However, the motivation for the Green Party was to have as much representation in as many government departments as possible. The situation was being additionally complicated because the Taoiseach, as part of this reshuffle, resulting from ongoing Green Party pressure, was to reduce the number of junior ministers.

Cowen's opening position was that he was not aware of the Ahern/Sargent agreement, nor would he be governed by it. Cowen's secondary argument was that if the number of junior ministers was being reduced, than the expected additional junior minister for the Greens should be part of that reduction. The Greens had expected an additional Minister of State before Bertie Ahern had increased, without consultation, their number to twenty. The party wasn't going to surrender that expectation now.

There was a bigger problem for the party too. The media got wind of the 2007 conversation within the Green parliamentary party on how a reshuffle might take place, especially concerning that shifting of portfolios from one Green TD to another. That the circumstances of such a reshuffle couldn't be forseen, controlled or acted on wouldn't get in the way of a story that whiffed of jobbery.

Green thinking had long promoted the idea of job sharing; of refreshing jobs through using new people. It isn't conventional thinking. Its airing tends to invite ridicule. It did in this case, as well as fuelling a feeling that Green TDs were dividing jobs, and the perks that go with them, amongst themselves. The contempt within the media and amongst the general public was being matched by a growing tension within the Green parliamentary party. The idea of Ciarán Cuffe becoming a Cabinet Minister with John Gormley standing aside, while remaining party leader, seemed, to many, ridiculous.

Several weeks of indecision, near infighting and public derision followed. Eventually, Cowen made his reshuffle. As a result, John Gormley and Eamon Ryan remained in the Cabinet with the jobs they had held. Other changes were minimal - Pat Carey at Community, Rural and Gaeltacht Affairs and Tony Killeen at Defence were the new faces. The Tánaiste, Mary Coughlan, swapped jobs with Batt O'Keeffe, placing her at Education and Science and him as Minister for Enterprise, Trade and Employment. Eamon O'Cuiv became Minister for Social Protection, replacing Mary Hanafin, who filled the vacancy at the Department of Arts, Sports and Tourism. Considering the time spent before the changes were made, an opportunity to radically reshape the government was missed.

The Greens did manage to win the argument about having an additional Minister of State. With the numbers reduced to fifteen from twenty, both Mary White and Ciarán Cuffe were appointed as junior ministers. Each was appointed to three departments, with Mary White being given Equality, Human Rights and Integration. The fact that Mary White was appointed to Equality came from a significant Green victory in taking Equality away from the Department of Justice during the most recent review of the programme for government negotiations.

Ciarán Cuffe was given responsibility for sustainable transport, planning and heritage, as well as Trevor Sargent's old food brief in the Department of Agriculture and Food. In that final role he would have a hard act to follow. Trevor had done an excellent job in the Department of Agriculture and Food – more farmers' markets took hold; organic production increased and significant initiatives in forestry were introduced. During the pork crisis of December 2008, Trevor's calm and assured performance outshone that of his senior Cabinet colleague. Most important of all was his influence within the Department itself; an influence that showed itself with the publication of the Food Harvest 2020 strategy document in 2010, which carried a significant green imprint. His dedication to the job was most marked when he became Minister for State. Having been a vegetarian, he reasoned that to represent the entire food industry he would have to become a meat-eater.

The 'rotating ministers' saga drew attention to the Green Party's attitude to political appointments. It was something towards which the party had sought to develop a different approach long before going into government. Throughout the term of government, the party put our ideas into action. About 50 Green Party members were nominated to public bodies. The party had set up an internal group to vet nominations. Sitting on this group were Mary White as Deputy Leader and Donal Geoghegan. The third member was an independent outsider with a human resources background.

Many key appointments, especially those made by Eamon Ryan, went to people without any Green Party background – Brendan Halligan to Bord na Móna, Lochlainn Quinn to ESB and Tom Savage to the RTÉ Authority were appointments that John Gormley would like to have seen go to others. No judicial appointments were made towards anyone with a Green background, despite the veneer that the appointment system for judges had become more independent. Names of suggested nominees were given, but the system constantly wheeled out 'reasons', sometimes spurious ones, as to why appointments were never made.

The Greens had secured a commitment in the review negotiations on legislation regarding future political appointments. Despite this, despite not availing of appointments on the scale that had been traditional to other political parties, and making more independent appointments than had been the norm, the party still found itself being pilloried as being no different from Fianna Fáil when it came to public appointments.

**

Trevor Sargent received a rapturous reception from Green Party members at the party's 2010 annual convention held in Waterford. Mary White and Ciarán Cuffe were also received well on foot of their new appointments. Outside the conference venue, the Tower Hotel, a welcome of a different sort greeted Green Party members. 2,000 people came to protest against continued Green Party participation in government.

A smaller proportion of those protesting were complaining against cuts, and the way in which those cuts had affected the community sector. The vast majority of protestors had been organised by a new lobby group, 'RISE' (Rural

Ireland Says Enough), a group established to react against animal welfare legislation that they argued was an attack on the values of rural Ireland.

An extremely well-resourced group, RISE focused its attention on two particular pieces of legislation - The Dog Breeding Establishment Bill and a Wildlife (Amendment) Bill that sought to outlaw the practice of stag hunting. It was this second bill that was to be the main impetus behind this group.

The Ward Union hunt, based in County Meath and North County Dublin, was the only stag hunt in the country. Its members contained many wealthy individuals. The master of the hunt was the developer Michael Bailey. When the reviewed programme for government agreed that a bill to outlaw the practice be published, the RISE campaign came into being. Skilfully run in public-relations terms, RISE's well-paid spokesperson created a narrative, using black propaganda, that came to be accepted as fact, especially in rural communities.

This narrative fostered a belief that all other blood sports were about to be banned. More insidious was the suggestion that the Greens had an anti-rural agenda.

The Dog Breeding Establishment Bill was the more progressed piece of legislation. In fact, it had started life under a previous Fianna Fáil Minister for the Environment, Dick Roche. Dealing with the regulation of puppy farms, where many unacceptable practices were occurring, the bill had not been a key Green demand in negotiations for government. However, John Gormley as the incoming Minister was happy to run with the bill and to strengthen it.

The bill was firstly introduced in the Seanad. The opposition parties saw the bill as a useful stick with which to beat the Greens, as well as a lever to create further division between the Greens and Fianna Fáil. Fine Gael tabled dozens of amendments, many of them contradictory. The Labour Party had also cynically opposed the bill, despite the play it was trying to make on winning the Green vote.

The debate in the Seanad was far longer than it needed to be. Fianna Fáil seemed happy to allow the bill to fester in the House. The greyhound industry was also lobbying, asking for separate and different regulation. In order to progress the Dog Breeding bill, John Gormley agreed to a separate bill to be introduced later dealing exclusively with greyhounds.

In the Dáil, the bill became a convenient vehicle for the Fianna Fáil back-benchers, like Mattie McGrath from Tipperary South, looking for a means of escape. The Labour Party was tying itself in knots over the issue. One of its TDs, Tommy Broughan, refused to oppose the bill. Labour had been receiving negative public reaction to its stance, which it then promptly reversed.

RISE, if its intent was to stop a ban on stag hunting coming into force, made a political miscalculation in putting so much of its lobbying efforts in to the Dog Breeding Establishments bill. The Wildlife (Amendment) Bill that followed moved through both Houses of the Oireachtas far more quickly.

The Green Party had little control over which bills were published when, or when parliamentary time was provided to debate them. Fianna Fáil's strategy seemed to have been to exaggerate the importance of these bills to the Greens and marginalise the party further. The Green view was that these were bills that had been agreed as part of a joint programme of government and they should have been dealt with quickly, allowing the opportunity for more important pieces of legislation to be considered.

One central piece of legislation was the Planning Bill; a piece of legislation that had been far too long in gestation. This bill would be the most radical overhaul of planning legislation since 1963. The Greens saw this as the most important piece of legislation that would be passed during its term of government. Changing the law to prevent inappropriate overdevelopment would help to avoid a repetition of the economic mess in which the country now found itself.

Along with the changes in the Building Regulations and improving the energy efficiency of new housing stock that had been agreed earlier, these would constitute the most significant achievements by the Greens. As these changes were long term in their effect and were less than tangible, the media, and consequently the general public, paid little attention to the passing of the Planning Act.

Another piece of legislation that was very important to the Greens was the Civil Partnership Bill. This too was taking far too long to process. Much of its delay was prior to its publication. For 18 months there had been an interminable series of meetings between Department of Justice officials, Ciarán Cuffe as the party's justice spokesperson with Roderic O'Gorman who undertook much of the work of behalf of the Greens on the bill.

Passage of the bill in the Dáil went perhaps too quickly, with insufficient attention being given to its contents. In the Seanad, though, a detailed debate occurred. Senator Ronan Mullen had organised a filibuster on the issue of Registrars having a conscientious right not to perform civil registrations. The Seanad gave as much time to debating the Civil Registrations Bill as it did to any other piece of legislation since 2007.

The filibuster involving Ronan Mullen and four other senators was coming close to derailing the bill. I insisted that a guillotine be used. There had been more than enough debate. I tried to articulate the reasons why this piece of legislation was so important to the Greens in my Second Stage speech:

> In these Houses of the Oireachtas we have the sometimes dubious privilege of passing much legislation. Some bills are quite regular in how they come to us and concern the daily running of the State. They are finance and social welfare legislation. Some bills are amendments to previous acts, seen through time and circumstance to be in need of change, or where the original tends to be seen as flawed. Some bills have an emergency nature, and we have seen more than enough in recent years dealing with the banking crisis and the financial position. Some legislation helps to define who we are as a society, and this is one such bill.
>
> As it is defining legislation, it does not come without controversy. There are those in our society who say: 'Thus far and no further', and there are those who quite legitimately have the right to expect that we need to go further. My party sees this as stepping-stone legislation, and there will be further bills to advance the continuing equality this legislation brings about. Nevertheless, it is a significant leap forward and we should mark the effect it will have on society.
>
> Most European countries have chosen to take a stepping-stone approach in this respect. In France, Germany, Switzerland, the Czech Republic, the United Kingdom and Finland, legislation is at the stage of civil partnerships. Spain, Portugal, Sweden, Norway, Iceland, Belgium and the Netherlands have legislation on full single-sex marriage. We should not see ourselves as

unique in this regard, and the process must be followed. I am proud that we are taking a significant step in that direction today.

As a society we must acknowledge our continuing immaturity in the area of sexuality. How sexuality is acknowledged, expressed, recognised and not celebrated in our society is something with which we must come to terms. For too many generations, many have had to endure a stigma that should never have been attached and, as legislators, we have ignored the problem for far too long. If there is anything in the debate we are having and the legislation we will pass today, it will be to remove from the shadows a stigma that should not have been placed to begin with. I can think of friends like Arthur Leahy in Cork who was involved in a television documentary in the 1970s, when it was first acknowledged that homosexuality existed in our country. It is a bit like the comment about The Late Late Show that sex did not exist before television.

We have come a long way since, but we still have a journey to travel. As a result of the repressed attitude to sexuality, where people were made to feel wrong if they had or expressed an inclination or felt part of a certain society, this bill only goes some of the way towards redressing the imbalance. I took part in recent gay pride parades in Cork, where 2,000 people marched, and in Dublin, where 22,000 people marched, and I finally got a sense, as a public representative, that we are emerging from those shadows and finally creating a society where people do not have to live in an undergrowth produced by people who for far too long expressed a vision of our society that was never a reality.

The sexual repression we have experienced in the past 100 or 150 years is not a natural Irish inclination, and is as far removed from the Brehon laws as could be.

Senator David Norris: Hear, hear.

Senator Dan Boyle: We are coming to terms with who we are as a people. In having this debate, and passing legislation, we should mark it as a celebration and an expression of pride. That it is not full equality or perfect is something I and my party acknowledge. That it needs to address elements such as children and the opinions of the Ombudsman for Children is most important. The contents of the bill will bring us forward, and I look forward to the day, as Senator Bacik has said, when the first ceremonies will be performed in the country.

I wish to address the question of conscience, as it has been expressed as a retarding effect on whether the legislation should pass. I acknowledge the presence of Senator Norris and the role he has played. In the game of social catch-up this country has played, and coming to terms with our repressed attitude to sexuality, we have waited far too long and experienced intervals far too wide. The decriminalisation of homosexuality occurred in the United Kingdom in 1967, but it was 26 years later that such legislation was passed here. It is almost 25 years since Senator Norris initiated his action in the European Court of Justice that helped to bring about the Irish legislation in 1993. Such an interval is far too long.

We can never have an Irish solution to an Irish problem with these issues again. This was a society where condoms had to be purchased on prescription if a person was married. How was that ever seen as a stepping-stone approach to a modern society? We have come a long way. I am concerned that some repressed attitudes remain. Some of these attitudes were expressed earlier today, while others were expressed in 1993. We must acknowledge that some of the negative comments made in 1993 are being reversed, and that the matters to which they relate have been addressed. The passage of this legislation will lead to a similar change of mindsets. The holding of ceremonies marking civil partnerships will create the momentum required to see to it that the full legislation required in this area is brought forward.

On the subject of conscience, I refer to John Fitzgerald Kennedy and his US presidential campaign of 1960. During that campaign he was subjected to a high level of criticism from religious fundamentalists about his Catholicism, how this would affect his role in office and how social policy in the United States would, if he were elected, reflect a particular Roman Catholic bias. During a speech he made in Dallas he stated:

I believe in a president whose religious views are his own private affair... and whose fulfilment of his presidential oath is not limited or conditioned by any religious oath, ritual or obligation... Whatever issue may come before me as president – on birth control, divorce, censorship, gambling or any other subject – I will make my decision in accordance with these views, in accordance with what my conscience tells me to be the national interest, and without regard to outside religious pressures or dictates.

The term 'aggressive secularism' has been used in the debate on the bill. I take the opportunity to out myself

189

as a secularist. I do not perceive secularism to be in any way aggressive. To me, it is the essence of tolerance.

Senator Ivana Bacik: Hear, hear.

Senator Dan Boyle: There are diverse views which need to be expressed – there must be circumstances in which they can be so expressed – and upheld. However, such views cannot be seen to dominate over those held by others. It is on that point that this debate should focus. We live in a society in which certain people's rights are not properly recognised within the legal system. These rights are only partially furthered by the legislation. When I hear it stated that conscience should be the guiding principle with regard to whether people should co-operate with the legislation when it has been passed by the Houses, I do not hear people speaking from conscience; rather I hear them referring to the right to discriminate.

Senator Ivana Bacik: Hear, hear.

Senator Dan Boyle: If we were to place this matter in the context of previous debates on social policy, the argument made in the past with regard to whether public officials should co-operate with people and whether people are divorced or cohabiting or whether they hold different religious opinions would again be made, but that is an Ireland which is dead and gone. It is an Ireland we need to leave behind.

It is left to me to make only one further point, which I will place in the context of a quote from Shakespeare's play Hamlet. I ask others to bear it in mind when they put us through the engaging debate in which we are going to partake for the remainder of today and tomorrow. The relevant quotation is 'Thus conscience does make cowards of us all'.

The passing of Civil Partnership Bill was significant. As the Minister responsible, Dermot Ahern scooped the plaudits. He certainly had made a journey from 1993, when he had made circumspect comments on the legislation on the decriminalisation of homosexuality introduced by Máire Geoghegan-Quinn.

It was frustrating to see the extent of the credit being given to Dermot Ahern, especially in the light of the difficulties that existed in bringing the legislation that far. As far as the Green Party was concerned this was a Green legislative achievement.

The legislative programme from the start of 2010 to the summer recess had been crammed with bills for which Green ministers had been responsible, or which were key priorities from the programme for government for the Green Party. A Planning Act; a Civil Partnership Act; a Wildlife (Amendment) Act and a Dog Breeding Establishment Act had all come through the Oireachtas. It was the first Oireachtas session since the Greens had entered into government, and green influence on the government was most obviously manifest.

Progress was also being made on other bills – the long awaited Climate Change Bill and a bill to create a directly elected Mayor for Dublin. Party confidence, which had been badly dented, was improving. In June John Gormley announced that a series of inquiries into planning matters at six local authorities would take place. Having earlier challenged development plans for Monaghan County and Ennis Town, he was motivated by a desire to clean up local government by removing any perception of poor planning practices. Nine months later his successor, Phil Hogan, decided that these inquiries were not worth pursuing.

12 | The End is Near

Through his contacts in Europe, John Gormley was being made aware of the extent of the Irish economic difficulties. Initially there seemed to be some slight improvement in the Irish debt situation after the measures taken in Budget 2011, but the unfolding crisis in Greece saw the Irish economy being dragged back into the mire.

The aim behind Irish government policy was to be able to return to the global money markets in January 2011. This was becoming less likely. John Gormley's contacts had convinced him that International Monetary Fund intervention in Ireland was inevitable. With this inevitability, he believed that the Green Party should prepare to leave government, which would be preferable to being in government when the IMF arrived.

After a successful period in passing legislation, John Gormley believed that this would have been the time for the Green Party to leave government. He stated his belief that without leaving government earlier the party risked losing all its seats and falling below the threshold where public funding would be given.

Eamon Ryan and I argued against him, believing that the budgetary strategy should be given more time to see if it could work. Added to this was our fear that to leave government then would be seen to be acting in the party's interest, when the country's interest required a will to remain and do what needed to be done.

That dichotomy was at the heart of Green Party's decision making during what would prove to be the final six months of government. It may have been the case that the ability to directly make decisions had already been taken from us.

In the unremitting gloom of everyday government decisions, Eamon Ryan spotted what he felt was an opportunity to deliver some good news. A review was taking place of the list of sporting events guaranteed to be viewed on terrestrial television. Eamon wanted to extend the list to include the Heineken Cup final. This had moved to satellite television a number of years previously, with a significant reduction of the number of people watching the event.

Eamon had reckoned without the vehement opposition of the Irish Rugby Football Union, which saw the move as an attempt to reduce the income of the sport. Middle-aged, middle-class men of South Dublin, a major part of Eamon's electorate, and who seemed to represent the IRFU at prayer, were particularly incensed at what was being proposed. It was another case of doing wrong for trying to do right.

The ever-growing distance between Fianna Fáil and the idea of accountability raised its head again in the issue of how the government chose to deal with a report of the Ombudsman, Emily O'Reilly, on the 'lost at sea' controversy. During the term of the previous government, while Minister for the Marine, Fianna Fáil's Frank Fahey had initiated a scheme to compensate owners of fishing vessels lost at sea.

There was subsequently seen to be many flaws with this scheme – how it was structured, how it was advertised and who ultimately benefitted from the scheme. It was this last point where much of the controversy was generated. All but one of the beneficiaries had County Galway addresses. This caused a great deal of dissension in fishing communities along the western seaboard.

With a brief to examine poorly functioning administration, the office of the Ombudsman undertook an investigation of this scheme. Since the office of the Ombudsman had been established over the previous thirty years, there had never been an incidence of a report from that office not being accepted by the government.

The issue was dealt with dismissively during a Dáil debate, and a half-hearted session of the Oireachtas Committee and Agriculture and the Marine. After being lobbied by a Donegal family that had been excluded from the scheme, Niall O'Brolcháin and I succeeded in having the issue re-introduced to the Oireachtas committee for further Oireachtas debate. The circumstances didn't change, but at least a more real consideration was given to the report.

The Green Party's own finances were not as healthy as they should have been. This was due to the Green Economy Expo that had been held in Croke Park in May. While many aspects of the event, designed to promote Green competence in economics, worked well, the anticipated revenue didn't arrive. Largely organised by Damian Connon and Nicola Cassidy, whose efforts deserved better, the event ended up making a considerable loss. John Gormley as party leader was particularly unhappy with the loss of resources that could have been available to meet the costs of the upcoming election.

For the government, Croke Park was to produce some better news. A major part of securing confidence in controlling the Irish budget deficit was in trying to show that the cost of public sector employment could be kept down. There was very little Green Party involvement in the process that led to the Croke Park agreement. We were surprised that agreement could be reached, and initially pleased when it had been. In retrospect, however, we should have recognised that the commitments made were vague and targets cited unrealistic.

Some relief for the government parties came when internal unhappiness with the leadership of Fine Gael came to the fore with an ill-considered challenge by Richard Bruton. It seemed that, despite not having the support of the majority of Fine Gael TDs, Enda Kenny hung on as its leader. He seemed to benefit from a public feeling that disapproved of this Fine Gael navel gazing. The public had decided that the existing parties of government would not be part of the next government. The public wanted the opposition parties to get their act together.

Normal service was soon resumed. If John Gormley had any sense of optimism that the Green Party might soon get a better bounce of the ball, it was knocked out of him by the 'white van man' saga.

As the Oireachtas went into summer recess, the advent of the silly season was announced with the publication of a news story in the *Irish Independent* on a supposed crack-down on van drivers using their vehicles for non-commercial purposes.

Within the Department of the Environment, it had been decided that renewal forms for motor taxation forms should be reviewed. It was a routine review, regularly done within the department, and was not initiated by any policy change or ministerial request.

The revamped form gave greater emphasis to the long-standing regulation that commercial van owners availing of a lower rate of motor tax could not do so if they used their vans for non-commercial reasons. When seized on by the *Irish Independent* story, this created an impression of people being pulled aside when taking their children to school or collecting an elderly relative.

The *Irish Independent* and, as a result, many members of the public, had no doubt who was responsible for this act of unfairness. That John Gormley had no knowledge was irrelevant because the story had gained its own momentum. It was something that people felt was likely to have the Greens behind it. The perception became reality for some people, regardless of the truth.

The silly season lasted longer than usual that Summer. Whimsical stories somehow gained legs, as much because people wanted to believe them as they trusted their veracity. As the political parties gathered for the pre-sittings think-in, another bizarre story took hold.

The Fianna Fáil parliamentary party think-in preceded that of the Greens. On the second day of the Fianna Fáil think-in, Brian Cowen was interviewed on the *Morning Ireland* radio programme. It wasn't the most assured of performances. Later that morning, Fine Gael's Simon Coveney, a constituency colleague of mine, tweeted: 'God, what an uninspiring interview by Taoiseach this morning. He sounded halfway between drunk and hungover and totally disinterested...' The tweet fed a hungry media. It also fed a stereotype of what many wanted to believe about Brian Cowen.

The Green parliamentary party think-in on that and the following day was overwhelmed and subsequently dominated by that tweet and this story, to the total exclusion of any positive story the Greens wanted to get out.

At the subsequent Cabinet meeting, Brian Cowen was apologetic to his ministerial colleagues. It was accepted that he shouldn't have done the interview, but was also felt that the media reaction was very over the top. That reaction caused huge damage to the reputation of both the Taoiseach himself and the country. US comic Jay Leno referred to the incident in his monologue on his highly watched *Tonight* programme.

Over the years, the think-in had been used as an opportunity to meet with and listen to people outside the Greens on the issues that we as a party were facing. People like David Begg of ICTU, John Fitzgerald of the ESRI, Father Sean Healy from Social Justice Ireland and Brendan Keenan, economics editor with the *Irish Independent*, all provided valuable input.

The Greens were looking forward to the coming parliamentary session because it was hoped that long-awaited pieces of legislation would finally see the light of day. In October, the Local Government (Mayor and Regional Authority of Dublin) Bill was published. Parallel to this, the Green Party started a campaign to convince people about the idea of a directly elected Mayor. The campaign was fronted by Paul Gogarty, who was also prepared to be the party's candidate should an election occur in Dublin. Neither Paul nor the party believed that it would be possible to win such an election. At best it would be seen as a profile-building exercise in advance of the general election.

Local government reform has always been a huge policy priority for the Greens. A Green Paper on the subject was released by John Gormley's department in early 2008. Having been drafted by officials in the department, it was fairly anodyne in its contents. A detailed consultation process followed in advance of a White Paper and a hoped-for bill.

Before this process was completed, Fianna Fáil sources leaked to the media that they had been successful in their goal of abolishing town councils. When a draft of the White Paper came before the Green parliamentary party, I felt that this had to be rejected. We were a party whose minimal presence in local government was now largely confined to town councils, besides which it ran against what we as a party believed should be the structure of local government.

What the Greens wanted was to increase the boundaries and the functions of town councils to create district councils. A new level of regional government would be created, we believed: Regional government that would achieve better economics of scale in the delivery of services through powers being devolved down to it downwards from national government and upwards from local government.

The effect of these reforms would be to question the purpose or usefulness of County Councils. These councils had been largely unreformed since their coming into being in 1899. Being some of the last remaining units of British administration in Ireland, far outlasting their British counterparts, questioning the future existence on county councils would have been a radical departure.

This disagreement delayed progress on the issues. There were other issues where Green Party objections would also cause delay. The reviewed programme for government committed the government to introducing water charges and a site value tax, both of which the Green Party felt were needed to have a sustainable system of local taxation.

Officials within the Departments of Finance and Environment wanted flat rate charges to be introduced for both. Greens believed that, once introduced, flat charges would remain. While believing that new charges/taxes were needed to bring about fairer taxation, this ongoing talking about taxes reinforced the belief that the Greens were a 'tax first' party.

The Greens wanted water meters before charges were introduced, so that householders would pay for excess use of water after exceeding a free household allowance. Having succeeded in agreeing a site value tax, the Greens insisted that the valuation system be put in place first before such a tax could be levied, again on equity grounds.

These were among the few areas where Green objections were causing delays. With most areas it was the Greens who were experiencing the delays. This was especially true of key pieces of legislation like the Climate Change Bill. It was clear that Fianna Fáil was adopting a 'drip drip' approach to the bill, raising reservations followed by ever more marginal progress. More frustrating still was the lack of progress on implementing the Aarhus convention of freedom of access to information on the environment. Ireland was the last country in Europe to have ratified, but not implemented, this convention. One by one, objections by different government departments were dealt with. The ultimate objection, however, seemed to be philosophical, emanating from the Attorney General's office.

Forty months into the life of the government, with time running out on so many levels, the Green party was juggling an ongoing economic crisis with seeking to progress key pieces of environmental legislation. There were other areas of policy and government to which the party, given its limited size and resources, just wasn't able to give sufficient attention.

Health was an area that had slid down the agenda. In an era of cutbacks, the ability to bring about positive change was limited. The Greens sought to have a medium-term/long-term effect on the Irish health care system. An Expert Group on Resource Allocation and Financing was set up in April 2009, and reported in the summer of 2011. The Greens had sought the establishment of this group, believing that alternative means of funding Irish health care should be investigated. The group produced an excellent report that was unfortunately ignored by the Irish media.

The need for a better method of funding Irish health care came even more into focus when the Irish government lost a European Court decision on the issue of community rating and the competition implications for health insurance companies.

One of the insurance companies, the Quinn group, was imploding – a direct result of machinations from the collapse of Anglo Irish Bank. A strange coalition of border Oireachtas representatives from Fianna Fáil and Fine Gael, and their Northern counterparts in Sinn Féin and the Democratic Unionist Party, pleaded for the ownership of the company to remain in the Quinn family's hands, asking that the company be given special treatment.

The new head of the Financial Regulator's office, Matthew Elderfield, wasn't having any of this. It was heartening to see a regulator actually regulating. It more than justified the Green Party's insistence that the new regulator should come from outside the jurisdiction.

Another issue that didn't get the attention from the Green Party that it should have was the issue of sexual abuse of children. The publication of the Ryan Report, one of what now was a series of reports into sexual abuse in the Catholic Church, horrified many.

The long made, yet still undelivered, promise that a constitutional referendum on inserting the rights of children was the reason why the Greens did not contribute to that debate in the way it should have been obliged to.

In the Seanad, small victories were achieved. The party had the opportunity of introducing Private Members legislation in the Upper House. Private Members legislation is restrictive. Any bill that has a cost implication for the State cannot be proceeded with. With these restrictions, the Greens sponsored a number of bills in the Seanad. One bill dealt with removing the right of forced treatment of electro-convulsive therapy, a bill that I was particularly happy to sponsor because of the intensive lobbying by John McCarthy of Mad Pride.

Another bill was to initiate an international treaty banning the use of depleted uranium weapons, as the government had already done in relation to cluster bombs. These were small victories, but they were not without some satisfaction.

In other respects, the Seanad was providing soap opera fodder that at least kept some of political media partially bemused. It had been reported that Fianna Fáil Senator Ivor Callely had inappropriately claimed travel expenses from a residence in West Cork while his political base had been in Dublin.

The Committee of Procedures and Privileges, compromising largely the leaders of the various Seanad groupings, decided to hold public hearings on the issue. I was a member of this committee as was Joe O'Toole, Fine Gael's Frances Fitzgerald and Labour's Alex White, while Fianna Fáil were represented by Denis O'Donovan and Camillus Glynn.

From the first day of the hearings, the questioning was aggressive, especially so from Alex White and Joe O'Toole. In asking my opening questions I at least tried to put it in some human context by suggesting that Ivor Callely and I shared some political similarities as we both lost Dáil seats at the previous election. He seized upon this, alluding that we shared personal similarities as well, implying that we had similar personal lives as well as similar political histories. Whatever warmth I had disappeared then.

The Fianna Fáil senators were neutral in their questioning, not wanting to be seen to 'do' one of their own. This extended to my announcing the decision of the committee that Ivor Callely be suspended without pay for thirty days. No Fianna Fáil senator wanted to make that announcement.

This decision was subsequently overturned in the courts; a decision that called into question the doctrine of separation of powers. The committee had erred, however. Much effort had been put into exposing the ethical transgressions of Ivor Callely, with not enough attention being given to whether the guidelines that existed allowed him to do that.

Some Green Party attention was also being given to another senator. If the government was to continue towards serving a full term, the nine Green Oireachtas members could play a role in the nomination process of the impending Presidential election. It wasn't rating very highly on the list of priorities but was still something that had to be followed up on. A meeting was arranged with David Norris about the possibility of such support. Along with the chair of the Green Party's National Council Roderic O'Gorman, I went to David Norris's house on North Great Georges Street.

Roderic, as well as being a party stalwart, would have been known to David Norris for the work he had done on the Civil Partnership Bill. He has the added advantage of being an attractive young man.

After ringing the doorbell at David Norris's house, he greeted us with a quip – 'I am honoured by a visit from the top and bottom of the Green Party!'

It at least provided temporary relief from the ongoing crisis. It was a circus to disguise the ever growing lack of bread.

13 | The Men In Black

The measures agreed in Budget 2010 initially seemed to be having the desired effect. Indicators seemed to going in the right direction. Then came the news from Greece.

Greece shouldn't have been directly comparable to Ireland. Whatever decision-making failings existed in Ireland, and undoubtedly there had been many, they didn't include falsifying economic data. The markets decided otherwise. Soon Ireland was following in Greece's wake, as would Portugal, with Spain and Italy all lumped together as the 'PIIGS'.

The Greek crisis was fast becoming a Euro crisis, an irony too rich for many of us in the Greens. We remembered being amongst the few challengers of, and the only political party to present arguments against, a common currency in the 1993 referendum on the Maastricht Treaty. Then the debate centred on then Taoiseach Albert Reynolds' claim that the IR£8 billion the country would receive in EU structural funds was reason enough to support the treaty.

The Greens had argued that rules leading to the formation of the Euro currency were inconsistent and would lead to a whole range of future difficulties. Not least of those was the danger of an asymmetric shock, where difficulties in a smaller economy would become exaggerated due to economic policy decisions being made for the wider currency zone. Seventeen years later, there would be no satisfaction in telling ourselves we were right.

In July 2010, the newly appointed Chief Executive of Anglo Irish Bank Mike Ainsley told an Oireachtas Committee that most of the then known bailout funding of €22 billion that was ploughed into Anglo Irish Bank would be irrecoverable. Both Ainsley and the bank's chairman Alan Dukes lobbied strongly for further funding to be pumped into the bank because they and their board considered that it would become viable. The Greens utterly rejected the proposal. As the party's finance spokesperson, I publicly poured cold water on the idea.

On September 8th, the Minister for Finance announced that Anglo Irish Bank would be restructured with a view to being phased out of existence. Later that month, in an interview with *The Irish Times*, Alan Dukes referred to me as 'that fucker Dan Boyle'. I wasn't surprised that he thought that way, but was surprised that The Irish Times chose to print it.

On foot of Brian Lenihan's announcement, the Governor of the Central Bank, Patrick Honohan, released long-awaited figures as to the likely total cost of the bank bailout. The figures were horrendous. The figure for Anglo Irish Bank alone was, at best, €29 billion with a possibility of the figure rising to €33 billion. The total cost of the bank bailout, Honohan asserted, could be as much as €50 billion.

Irish Nationwide Building Society, the plaything of Michael Fingleton, would end up costing the Irish taxpayer €5.4 billion; almost as much as Bank of Ireland and Allied Irish Bank, despite having a capitalisation and a turnover far less than those institutions.

The news of the true scale of the Irish banks' recapitalisation needs was unexpected, and sent the money markets into a spin. Bond yields for Irish government bonds soared above the 7% figure deemed to be unsustainable. Bond sales that were expected in October and then November were withdrawn.

The Irish government tried to maintain confidence by stating that Ireland's borrowings were sufficient to ensure cash reserves were on hand that would take the country well into 2011 in terms of government spending. This was true, but seemed to do little to assure the markets. Even so, the hope was that the country could be able to return to the money markets in January.

Before that, the activities of the government were to become subject to ever growing international intervention. At the start of November, the first visitor was Olli Rehn, the European Union Commissioner for Economic and Monetary Affairs. EU support was dependent on reaching agreement on a four year budgetary strategy, the details of which Rehn's visit was meant to inform. Who was informing whom was a moot question. As a party, we needed to know the real extent to which the European Commission was putting pressure on the Irish government, but similarly we needed to know how well the Commission understood the political realities of the Irish economic situation.

Rehn was to spend a day engaging in a series of whistle-stop meetings with political parties and the social partners. His day started early with a meeting with Brian Cowen and Brian Lenihan. In a nearby room in the Taoiseach's section of Government Buildings, John Gormley, Eamon Ryan and I waited. When he arrived, he presented himself as the technocrat he was. The atmosphere was businesslike. John sought to lighten the mood by making reference to Rehn's soccer playing past, but bonhomie would not be the mood of the meeting. Rehn went on to say that European Commission support for Ireland depended on 'structural changes' being made to the Irish economy. We asked what structural changes the Commission had in mind. He cited the example of the level of the minimum wage, which was high in European terms. Mention was made of the corporation tax rate, but this, unlike the minimum wage, was not being insisted on.

At least, it was our belief that a change in the minimum wage was being insisted on. Later, after the change had reluctantly been made, the Irish Congress of Trade Unions was to receive a letter from Rehn claiming that he had not asked that this change be made. This is the danger of un-minuted meetings being held without officials.

Where Rehn was supportive was in his and the Commission's belief that the strategy being followed by the Irish government was essentially correct. If continued, there would be no need of direct intervention from the European Central Bank or the International Monetary Fund. That meeting was being held on the first week of November 2010.

From the start of November, the Green parliamentary party began having near daily, and often several, meetings. On November 2nd, a meeting concentrated on election preparations. Asked what was felt should be the main theme that the Greens should emphasise in an election, Green Oireachtas members parted ways.

Niall O'Brolchain said that the relevance of the party should be stressed. Trevor Sargent believed that the emphasis should be on shedding the Fianna Fáil connection. Mary White felt that we should emphatically state that the Greens should never work with Fianna Fáil again. Ciarán Cuffe wanted Jobs and the Environment to be stressed. Mark Dearey suggested a slogan that 'The recovery will be Green'. Press officer Damian Connon suggested that the opening theme for the election campaign should be 'change the government, keep the experience'.

Eamon Ryan believed that the party needed one simple, accessible messsage. In contrast to other members of the parliamentary party he said that it would be difficult to talk about a place in the next government. He further asked whether it was really credible that the Greens detach completely from Fianna Fáil having stayed the course for this long. It was better, he felt, that the party present itself as the party that can and has provided competent governance. The Green experience of government, in his opinion, should be the greatest selling point.

On the issue of preparedness, some candidates, Ciarán Cuffe and Trevor Sargent, already had election literature and posters ready. As the most experienced and successful election campaigner in the party, Trevor stressed the importance of the party being ready as and when an election would be called.

Trevor Sargent continued to argue that the Fianna Fáil relationship would have to be addressed. For him, it had to be said that they weren't the Greens' preferred coalition partner and they stopped Greens accomplishing what we wanted to be done. The message should be that we wanted to be more radical now that we can be. In this he was strongly supported by Mary White.

Mark Dearey warned of what many of us had come to realise: that there would be retribution from the electorate, whose desire to damage Fianna Fáil would steamroll the party. Trevor Sargent wanted the party to play to perceived strengths by bringing forward people who have benefited from the Greens being in government.

Which sector of the electorate the party should concentrate on also brought divisions in the parliamentary party. Mark Dearey believed that there was no point in focussing on the traditional Green vote. Mary White thought that many of these voters had been lost already, particularly young mothers.

The discussion at the meeting synthesised that the major issues on which the party should focus would be education, planning and banking reform.

In closing the meeting, Donal Geoghegan, half in jest, suggested that it was time for a stunt – another 'Rumble in Ranelagh' perhaps?

This was a meeting about election preparedness. Other than John Gormley, who had already stated his reservations, no other member of the parliamentary party wanted an election to be held just yet. Within twenty-four hours, the parliamentary party was to meet again for a reason that would make an election ever more likely.

**

On 3rd November 2010, the High Court made a ruling on an action taken by Sinn Féin Senator Pearse Doherty over the delay in holding a Donegal South West By-Election, where a vacancy had existed since June 2009 when Pat 'The Cope' Gallagher had been elected to the European Parliament.

Fianna Fáil's reluctance to hold this, and other by-elections, had been a source of embarrassment to the Greens. The High Court decided that there had been an unreasonable delay in the holding of this by-election, which was a direct breach of the 1992 Electoral Act.

It was obvious that Fianna Fáil, through the Attorney General, would argue that the High Court decision should be appealed to the Supreme Court, and also argue that the by-election should continue to be delayed until such an appeal was heard.

At our parliamentary party meeting I argued that, regardless of any appeal, we should insist on the immediate holding of the by-election. In this I was strongly supported by Trevor Sargent. Our Clare Councillor Brian Meaney had already made a public statement stating that the by-election couldn't be delayed any further.

The meeting was interrupted by my going out onto the plinth in Leinster House with Trevor as Party Whip to announce that we wanted the by-election to be held immediately.

The reconvened parliamentary party met again to discuss election preparations with a renewed intensity. Wider issues, such preparation of a manifesto, were discussed. Parallel to these discussions, we created a checklist of where certain pieces of legislation stood. There remained an impasse with the White Paper on Local Government. Difficulties were also discussed with the Nurse and Midwives Bill. Between election preparations and an ever-deteriorating economic situation it was becoming increasingly difficult to keep on top of the day-to-day business of government.

On 6th November, the parliamentary party met again in the aftermath of the visit of Olli Rehn. The focus of attention was on the upcoming budget. The Department of Finance was proposing that changes in education, which had been defeated by the Greens during the review of the programme of government, should now occur. Increases in third-level registration fees, increasing the pupil-teacher ratio and cutting back capitation grants were the measures being considered. This was in the context of demographic expansion resulting in the education budget being the only large spending department that would have an increasing allocation.

We had to make a decision as to whether we could accept these proposed changes. The pupil-teacher ratio had to be maintained as far as we were concerned. We could accept a rise in the registration fee. Eamon Ryan was prepared to use some of his department's budget to maintain capitation levels. Having suffered badly on the issue of education in the 2009 elections, we were determined to be on the right side of the issue now.

The prevailing view of the parliamentary party was that if there wasn't to be an election soon, there would certainly be an election by March. The public statements by Olli Rehn about the need for consensus in the Irish political system also had the effect of concentrating our collective mind. John Gormley believed that consensus on the budget with Fine Gael and Labour on the basis of agreeing an early election date was something towards which he should work.

Updates were given on key pieces of legislation, and some movement seemed to be happening on the Climate Change Bill, although by now we knew that supposed advances were carrots being offered by Fianna Fáil when it was felt that the Greens were nervous about remaining in government.

The bill on corporate donations seemed to be hitting a brick wall, with the Attorney General insisting that it was unconstitutional. John Gormley was admitting that the party had erred in not asking more questions on the issue of appointing an Attorney General in 2007.

On 11th November, a key meeting was organised between the Green Party, the Minister of Finance and his officials. It took place at the Department of Finance, and was to deal with the final areas of disagreement relating to the Budget being finalised. Representing the Greens was John Gormley, Eamon Ryan, Donal Geoghegan and I. With Brian Lenihan was Kevin Cardiff, the Secretary General of the Department, and senior officials Derek Moran and

Robert Wall, responsible respectively for the taxation and the spending aspects of the Budget.

All present were aware that this Budget would be the most severe in the history of the State. Despite that, Lenihan's mood was incredibly upbeat. It was hard to know if it was bravado or that his ebullience was linked with a positive effect from his medication. His mood contributed to a meeting that was held largely in good humour. Green concerns on education were addressed. Commitments were given on abolishing the remaining contentious tax reliefs.

On one issue, the Greens were to receive no satisfaction. Conscious that the Budget would disproportionately affect the lowest paid, the party wanted movement on the issue of refundable tax credits – the making of cash payments to the lowest paid for not being able to avail of the tax credits allocated to them. The Greens saw this being introduced on a low-level, phased basis – €100 per qualifying worker per year. Brian Lenihan was sympathetic to this proposal and saw merit in its introduction. He preferred to see it introduced on a larger scale, which meant that it would wait for a later budget. I wasn't happy with this, but even less happy with the reaction from the Department of Finance officials, one of whom directly said there will not be an integration of taxation and social welfare systems. I was surprised at the vehemence of this reaction, angered at an official being so directly involved in the making of policy and depressed by the reluctance of the Department to bring about change.

At the end of a lengthy meeting, Brian Lenihan started to speak to an issue that hadn't been raised. 'You may have heard rumours that IMF officials are working within the Department. They are there, but they are not looking at the books. They are examining an issue relating to public service pensions.' We hadn't asked. What raising the issue had done was plant an idea in our heads that hadn't been there.

Those doubts were to predominate in the days that followed. In Seoul, South Korea, a G20 summit was being held that weekend. At a gathering of the world's twenty largest economies, Ireland was being represented through the European Commission.

Ireland's situation was obviously being discussed at the summit, but, without direct representation, reacting to media reports was proving difficult. Among those media reports from Reuters and the BBC were stories that the IMF was about to intervene in Ireland. The sources of these stories were either from the German government or from the European Central Bank or both.

The intent behind these stories was that Ireland needed to be made an example of. What wasn't being said was that the IMF could not directly intervene in any country, but would have to be invited in by a country that was in need of assistance. This seemed to be a co-ordinated attempt to force Ireland's hand.

The media stories became ever more persistent over the weekend. Cabinet Ministers Noel Dempsey and Dermot Ahern together denied there was any truth in these stories. While both were subsequently derided for their sense of certainty, it was clear that neither knew of impending IMF arrival. That weekend on social networking sites I was saying the same thing. In the wider media, Green representatives chose to say nothing because, in truth, we did not know what there was to know.

On Monday 15th, the Green parliamentary party held a meeting by teleconference. All of us were looking for confirmation on the media reports. John Gormley had contacted Brian Cowen, and was given assurances that the IMF had not been applied to. Sovereign debt was not affected according to Cowen, but the additional banking debt being subsumed was causing a difficulty; a difficulty that was drawing attention to the country that would concern and may involve the interest of the IMF. A meeting with Brian Lenihan that afternoon would tell a broader story.

The Green Parliamentary party was due to meet the following day for another of the election preparation meetings. John Gormley reported that a statement had been agreed with Brian Lenihan on the current state of play. This statement admitted for the first time that discussions had been entered into, but not with the intention of entering into a loan facility or programme.

It was merely a holding statement. The uncertainty still existed, and would continue to grow. In the Green Parliamentary party, talk refocused onto election preparations for an election that was becoming ever more likely. Concerns persisted about the progress, or lack thereof, on key pieces of legislation. Most discussions centred around the question of to what extent any future relationship between the Green Party and Fianna Fáil should exist.

The following exchanges from that meeting give a sense of the differing views that were held in the parliamentary party on this:

Colm O'Caomhanaigh (Party General Secretary): We need to decide on ruling Fianna Fáil in or out.
Dan Boyle: We can't rule them out as part of a national government.
Paul Gogarty: We already ruled them out in 2007, and then went in with them, so we have no credibility on this question at this stage. They are no different to Fine Gael or Labour.

Niall O'Brolcháin: I agree with Paul. No credibility on this front, so no point in making a big deal of it.

Mary White: I disagree completely! We have to rule them out. They have cost us so many votes already by association. We will be asked this question directly on the doorsteps and in the media and we need a coherent answer.

Dan Boyle: Can we say that our experience tells us that it would be difficult to work with them again?

Colm O'Caomhanaigh: Waste of time ruling them out, it doesn't ring true at this stage.

Eamon Ryan: It's not credible and would be seen as a cynical move on our part. We could cause ourselves damage by focussing on it too much.

Donal Geoghegan (Programme Manager): We'll look at options for ensuring that the electorate understands the distance between us and Fianna Fáil.

That evening, John, Eamon and I attended a meeting of the party's National Executive Council. The concern of the party's activists was obvious. However, there was general support for the approach being taken by the parliamentary party.

On Wednesday 17th, the parliamentary party held its third meeting in as many days. By now, the realisation was dawning that with regard to the IMF it was no longer a question of 'if' but 'when' we entered a programme. The impact of this eventuality was what the parliamentary party talked about. These contributions give a sense of what Green TDs and Senators were thinking at this time:

John Gormley: In the next week we could have entered the facility. If this is the case, are we happy to continue on?

Ciarán Cuffe: It's not entirely black and white. If the IMF is running the economy then we have lost our mandate as a government, but should still attempt to pass the budget and present the four year plan to the people. Hold out for election in early January.

Trevor Sargent: If we go into an election next week we would wreck the country.

John Gormley: The country is already wrecked! The IMF is here!

Eamon Ryan: We need calm now. It would be irresponsible to go now. Getting the budget through is of greatest importance now. The terms of the deal will be largely in line with what is already being done.

Dan Boyle: We have painfully few options at this stage. We need to see what is being proposed before we can make a decision. But if we cannot determine the budget then what is the point in staying?

John Gormley: It's so hard to get to the truth; very difficult to get a clear picture at Cabinet.

Paul Gogarty: The parliamentary party is being left in the dark.

Niall O'Brolchain: If we are leaving we need to have a very clear reason for doing so, and at the moment we don't have enough information.

John Gormley: This scenario takes far too much explaining. It would be better to go on Fianna Fáil not playing ball on salaries, expenses etc.

Ciarán Cuffe: The general public don't want panic; they want and need stability right now.

Mark Dearey: It all depends on the conditions of the deal. If what is proposed is a complete anathema to the values of this party then we have to go. We have to cross the floor.

Mary White: It would be very damaging to leave in panic at this moment. We would be accused of not being able to handle the situation.

Trevor Sargent: The conditions will determine future moves. When will we know what they are?

Eamon Ryan: Barrosa is to talk to the Taoiseach. In the meantime, we should seek Fine Gael involvement. We should do some work with them in the background.

Trevor Sargent: We should have common purpose with the opposition. Remain calm and work towards an election in February.

Ciarán Cuffe: Reaching out to Fine Gael is a good approach. Statesmanlike behaviour from us is what's needed.

Paul Gogarty: There's a good chance that Fine Gael won't go for it. What we need is a well managed exit from government now.

Mary White: My gut instinct says not to pull the plug just now. We have to be masters of our own destiny. We have to put the country first.

John Downing, Assistant Government Press Secretary, advised that the Green silence on the issue couldn't be maintained any longer. Eamon met with the media after that day's Cabinet meeting saying that the Green Party's continuation in government had always been dependent on doing what best for the country. The Greens wanted to see real reform and the budget passed.

On the morning of the 18th, the Green Party's National Executive Council held a special meeting. The predominant feeling was that the party should leave government and support a budget from the opposition benches. The idea of holding a special convention of party members was not thought practical, although the indications were that three or four constituency groups were talking about trying to bring one about.

At the parliamentary party meeting that followed, John Gormley read the contents of a letter that he had received from Brian Cowen addressing concerns that existed on key pieces of legislation. In this letter Brian Cowen gave assurances that the Corporate Donations and Climate Change bills would be proceeded with. His response on waste levy legislation was less certain. Debate in the parliamentary party continued on the questions of whether, how and if the party should withdraw from government:

Mary White: How will our pulling out be perceived by EU leaders? Voting for the budget and motions of confidence, even from the opposition benches, will still be perceived as propping up Fianna Fáil.

Trevor Sargent: We're being strung along because of our interest in policy. Fianna Fáil don't understand this and see it as our weak spot. We need to make a statement to say that we support the budget and the four year plan and that our support will end after the Finance Bill has been passed. We need to be seen to be decisive and to call the shots.

John Gormley: Why do we have a duty and Fine Gael and Labour don't?

Paul Gogarty: It's now looking less and less likely that we'll see movement on our key areas. The plan now should be to come back on 7th January, vote for the budget and the morning after say that we have done our duty and leave government.

John Gormley: We can't support a budget that doesn't contain real reform on salaries, pensions etc.

Mary White: We have to push Cowen to the limit, otherwise he just doesn't listen.

Donal Geoghegan: Caution. Look at the facts: Cowen's letter is not stringing us along, He is very clear on three out of four points here. Waste is a problem, but we're dealing with it.

Ciarán Cuffe: We need to flesh out in detail all scenarios.

Donal Geoghegan: We need to know exactly why we're leaving and be able to communicate that reason effectively.

John Gormley: I know why we're leaving! We can't work with them any more.

Dan Boyle: What about the following – submit resignation letters, he accepts and goes to the park, he doesn't accept and we get a better deal.

John Gormley: What is our bottom line? His response is not acceptable. Under what circumstances will we vote against the budget? Political reform? Salaries?

Mary: It's not good to make decisions while worked up. Put it to Cowen. He has to believe that we are going to go. We need a response by this evening.

Paul Gogarty: Why can't we publish the Climate Change Bill now?

John Gormley: It's still not ready to go.

Paul Gogarty: Then that's entirely our fault.

Eamon Ryan: Step back for a moment. John is right to push ahead with Cowen. Everyone be careful what they say publicly. We don't want to do the country any more damage.

That morning, speaking on *Morning Ireland*, the Governor of the Central Bank, Patrick Honohan, confirmed that discussions were being held with the IMF with a view to the country making an application for a large loan. The country was edging ever nearer the long-feared inevitability.

On Friday 19th, the fifth Green parliamentary party meeting in five days was held. The debate continued with the same questions being asked:

> *Eamon Ryan: We need to bear in mind that we're at the centre of a crisis in the Euro. We have difficult decisions to make in the coming days. There is no easy analysis. The Parliamentary party must be as informed as soon as possible when making a decision. There will be a meeting with Lenihan tomorrow on the four year plan.*
> *Trevor Sargent: We need to get a message out to say we're going. When can we do that?*
> *John Gormley: We will see very ugly scenes here soon, civil disorder – after the budget and into the new year.*
> *Mary White: Media and opposition would be extremely critical if we jump ship now. We have to pass the Budget.*
> *Mark Dearey: The announcement that we will be going is extremely important. The NEC is encouraged by progress made on policies. They could be won over by further progress.*

Members of the party's National Executive then joined the meeting. They were Roderic O'Gorman (Chair of National Council – the party's policy-making arm), Gary Fitzgerald (co-ordinator NEC), Stiofán Nutty (former Party General Secretary), Phil Kearney (long time party activist), Martha Dalton (Chair of the Young Greens), Cadogan Enright (Northern Ireland councillor), Edel Hackett (Deputy Co-ordinator) and Andrew Murphy (former Chair of the Young Greens).

John Gormley brought the group up to date, saying that if we were to go now we would be severely criticised for bringing further instability to an already unstable situation. Decisions on the conditions of the deal were going to be made over the weekend, with confidence votes held the following week. Our legislation would be seen as irrelevant by the majority of people at this stage. We were staying for the moment.

Edel Hackett raised the point that Fianna Fáil's determination to cling to power was a problem. 'How long can we continue to support them?' She asked.

Roderic O'Gorman said that if we get all four key issues delivered on then we could stay, but that the Attorney General remained a problem.

Andrew Murphy believed that ending now would be damaging, but a decision on when to leave needed to be made.

Cadogan Enright stated that the party will be hammered no matter when it left government, so getting policies through was more important than distancing from Fianna Fáil.

Paul Gogarty argued that the party tried to put push on for legislation to be passed before Christmas, but this hasn't worked. Not enough civil servants were available to draft, so external drafting should be done. But the party still had a moral obligation to pass the budget.

On Saturday, further meetings of the parliamentary party confirmed a course of action once a decision on the IMF had been announced. On Sunday 21st, Brian Lenihan telephoned EU Commissioner Olli Rehn to inform him that Ireland did intend to approach the IMF and the ECB about entering the support facility. By Monday 22nd, that news would be publicly known. The Green parliamentary party met once again to work out what by now was a largely predetermined response. It was obvious to all that our participation in government was quickly coming to an end. What we needed to work out was the how and the when. We worked collectively on a press statement from John that would be read out at a press conference later that day. The statement read as follows:

> The past week has been a traumatic one for the Irish electorate. People feel misled and betrayed.
>
> The Green Party believes three things must be done in the coming two months to safeguard the future prosperity and independence of the Irish people.
>
> These are:
>
> - Producing a credible four year plan to show we can make our Budgets balance by 2014;
>
> - Delivering a Budget for 2011; and
>
> - Securing funding support from the EU and IMF, which will respect vital Irish interests and restore stability to the Euro area.
>
> We have always said that our involvement in government would only continue as long as it was for the benefit of the Irish people. Leaving the country without a government while these matters are unresolved would be very damaging and would breach our duty of care.
>
> But we have now reached a point where the Irish people need political certainty to take them beyond the coming two months. So, we believe it is time to fix a date for a general election in the second half of January 2011.
>
> We made our decision last Saturday after a long series of meetings.
>
> Since entering government in June 2007, we in the Green Party have worked to fix and reform the economy.

It has been difficult. We have taken tough decisions and put the national interest first.

We cannot go back and reverse the property bubble and the reckless banking which we consistently spoke against and opposed. Nor can we control the market turmoil which has afflicted the Euro area.

We have taken extensive measures to recognise the losses and stabilise our banking system. However, it is now clear we need further measures to give market confidence about our banks and public finances.

We are now discussing ways of restoring stability to the banking system with the support of our European colleagues and the IMF. We have to ensure that the terms of any such support are in the interests of the Irish people and the wider Euro area.

The timeframe for achieving a four year plan, Budget 2011 and a good outcome from IMF/EU talks is very short.

These matters must at this stage take priority ahead of everything else.

Despite our difficulties and disappointments, I believe we can get out of this situation. We must all work together to ensure the best outcome for everyone.

On agreeing the text of the statement, we talked about the need to inform the Taoiseach. While it was agreed that the Taoiseach should be – had to be – informed, it was felt that 45 minutes' notice was all that should have been required, lest attempts were made undermine the Greens' wish to get our views out first.

Attempts to even give this type of notice were stymied when John Gormley phoned the Taoiseach, only to learn that he was in the middle of an interview with his local radio station Midlands Radio 3. The Taoiseach's immediate response given to John Gormley was one of disappointment.

With that call made, the Green Parliamentary party made its way to the Audio/Visual room in Leinster House, where the assembled members of the media were awaiting the statement.

The parliamentary party was being joined by an additional member. Paul Gogarty had brought his daughter Daisy with him that day, having had some childcare difficulties. While there has always been a tolerance of children at Green events, many members of the parliamentary party were not comfortable with Paul having Daisy with him on the podium at the press conference, although none, other than Mark Dearey, said so to him. It detracted from the optics of the situation.

There was surprise among the media at the contents of the Green statement. An expectation had grown with a shared media analysis that there would never be a circumstance in which the Greens would choose to leave government. But there was also confusion with the statement, especially the section dealing with a likely election date. The line calling for the date of an election to be fixed in January created an expectation that the Greens wanted the election to be held in January.

The reality was that the Greens would have little control over the drafting of the Finance Bill. There would be an expectation that the Dáil could be recalled early, and that a Finance Bill could pass all stages by some time in January, to be followed a general election campaign. As this was my formulation, I take full responsibility for the confusion it caused. It even confused the Green Party press office.

In retrospect, it probably wasn't the correct approach. Resigning from government, removing expectations of having legislation passed and voting for a Budget and Finance Bill from the opposition benches probably would have been a better approach.

The press conference out of the way, John Gormley went to meet the Taoiseach, who was less benignly disposed than he had been in his phone call. He was not happy. He was displeased at the level of notice he was given, as he felt that something could have been worked out. He didn't look for John's resignation.

For the rest of the day, rumours abounded. Word filtering from Government Buildings was that the Taoiseach wanted to go to the President and call and election, but he was being talked down by his Fianna Fáil Cabinet colleagues. Brian Lenihan, having earlier been doorstepped and talking down the possibility of problems with the government, was also furious with the actions of the Greens. Discontent among Fianna Fáil back-benchers seemed to be rising. Independent TDs supporting the government were talking up their own demands.

Leinster House was surrounded by the media. The international media camped on Merrion Street. Since the G20 summit, Ireland and its budgetary difficulties had become the number one world news story. I was the Green pushed forward by the press office to talk with the international media. Interviews with Bloomberg, Reuters, BBC Radio 4 and France 24 followed in quick succession. While waiting to have a live interview with Jon Snow on Britain's *Channel 4 News*, a newsflash was made that the Taoiseach was to make a statement from the steps of Government Buildings.

I was convinced that he would be announcing his intention to calling a general election. I was astounded when he seemed to agree with the Green Party's analysis that this government was now winding down, that important work remained to be done in bringing forward a four year budgetary plan, a budget and a Finance Bill.

The following day, the business of government continued in an almost surreal way. A number of Ministers, including Eamon Ryan, were travelling to Northern Ireland for a series of meetings with their Assembly counterparts. It was not the most comfortable of days for Eamon.

The decision to approach the IMF was not without effect within the Green Party. Party Co-ordinator Gary Fitzgerald tendered his immediate resignation. Gary had been a strong and committed opponent of the party's approach to NAMA. He accepted the view that the majority of the party had expressed. He had become a key volunteer in the day-to-day workings of the party. His resignation, on the grounds that many of us felt that the introduction of the IMF was a political humiliation, removed from the party an important, honest, critical voice.

A parliamentary party meeting was held on Thursday 25th to review the events of the week. Aside from the regular checklist of the status of legislation and preparations for the Budget, the results of constituency opinion polls undertaken on behalf of the party were revealed. The polls were conducted in John Gormley's constituency of Dublin South East and the Carlow/Kilkenny constituency of Deputy Leader Mary White. They did not make for pleasant reading. An 8% figure was recorded in Dublin South East, with a 7% figure being listed for Carlow/Kilkenny, meaning that a seat could not be won in either place.

The Four Year Budget Plan was also announced on that day. The media launch was conducted by Brian Cowen, Brian Lenihan and John Gormley, at least giving the appearance of a government in place working together. The contents of the plan gave no reason for comfort. It committed to a €15 billion adjustment in the budget over the four year period with an initial €6 billion to follow in a number of weeks.

What we were hearing from the talks with the IMF and the ECB was not reassuring. The opening percentage for the package being offered was 7%. This was not much below the rate available to the country on the international money markets. There wasn't any doubt that there was a huge punitive element attached to all this. The position of the ECB seemed far more hard line than that of the IMF, who seemed to be playing the role of 'good cop' in the negotiations.

The IMF also seemed to be taking a more supportive position on the question of defaulting on unsecured bondholders. The ECB with the European Commission, undoubtedly heavily influenced by the position of the German government, would not countenance such a move.

Completing a week that the government would want to forget, on Friday the Donegal South West by-election was held. When the votes were counted, the inevitable result was reached. Sinn Féin's Pearse Doherty had won. In the few remaining days of the 30th Dáil he would become an effective opposition irritant against the government.

In the days that followed the Four Year Plan launch, John Gormley did an excellent job in knitting Fine Gael and Labour into accepting the €15 billion and €6 billion figures as the figures that needed to be met by whoever found themselves in government in the years to come. The opposition parties still gave themselves the freedom to vote against the budget, as well as promoting a fiction that while they accepted the overall figures they would choose different routes in reaching those goals.

The finalising and agreeing of the facility package also helped to concentrate minds. €85 billion, with the Irish government contributing €17.5 billion, largely through from the

National Pension Reserve Fund, was the price to be paid. The average interest rate at 5.83% remained onerous.

The elements of the package should have contributed to a wider debate on the nature of the country's financial difficulties. €35 billion of the package was towards a resolution of the banking crisis, the issue that consumed practically all of the public attention. The bulk of the package at €50 billion was dedicated to trying to sort out the national finances, which had been wrecked by years of overspending and undermining of the tax system.

The political debate, such as it was, centred around how poor a deal the Irish government had secured. Thankfully, we had very little input into the negotiations. The Irish team of Patrick Honohan, Governor of the Central Bank, Kevin Cardiff, Secretary General of the Department of Finance, and John Corrigan, Chief Executive of the National Treasury Management Agency, represented the country well in dealing with the IMF's Ajai Chopra and his team.

Where there were political considerations, they concerned how this would play into the future. The hope, if not the expectation, would be that interest rates could be lowered, and more importantly that some of the debt could be written off.

The atmosphere between Fianna Fáil and the Greens had cooled considerably since the events of November 22nd. The spinning seemed designed to keep the government going and the Greens within it. The lack of specificity on the election date was translated by some Fianna Fáilers as meaning April or maybe even May by the time the Finance Bills would have passed all stages in both Houses of the Oireachtas. It never meant that to us; at worst it would have meant an election in early March. Some more fanciful Fianna Fáilers even speculated that the Greens might change their minds about leaving government if progress was being seen to be made on legislation. Again, that was never the case.

Signals coming from the Cabinet seemed to advance this theory. Progress was being made on pieces of legislation that had been stalled for months. In coming weeks, Cabinet approval, publication and the provision of parliamentary time would become possible for several pieces of Green-sponsored legislation.

Outside of the programme for government, the Green Party was presenting other legislation that was certain not to get any parliamentary time. Embarrassed at the lack of legal action against bankers, I drafted a bill on Economic Treason. Bills to change the Constitution could not be introduced in the Seanad. Trevor Sargent agreed to introduce the bill in the Dáil.

Useful initiatives that had been started by the Green Party were being lost in the unusual political circumstances that were prevailing. In November, the final report of the Expert Group on Mortgage Arrears and Personal Debt reported, to general indifference. The group was established because of work done by Eamon Ryan, who had recognised that addressing bank debt should be matched with a similar government approach to personal debt.

Responding to opposition taunts while answering questions in the Dáil chamber, John Gormley likened being in government to being in an asylum. It wasn't the most politically correct formulation, but we all understood what he meant.

Most attention continued to be drawn to the contents of the Budget. The Green Party continued to argue with the Minister for Finance on a number of issues. We believed that, given the scale of adjustment that was needed, some humanising elements were essential. We had argued for a refundable tax credit. We pushed for some kind of wealth tax, but we particularly looked for a significant cut in politicians' pay. We thought that the first two elements would be unlikely. We were amazed at the argument being advanced by Lenihan that significant cuts in politicians' pay weren't possible because TDs would be less likely to support a difficult budget if their wages were being reduced!

Independent TD Michael Lowry was laying down his own conditions for supporting the Budget. He wanted the tax treatment of casinos to be done differently to enhance the likelihood of a project in Tipperary. The Greens would not support that. Lowry was offered a non-binding report with no legislative change.

The Budget on 7th December was presented with the minimum of fuss. Reaction to it, because of all that preceded it, was quite muted. None of that changed the reality: the budget was the longest suicide note in Irish political history.

14 | The End of The End

As 2011 came into view there was a sense of relief with Green Party Oireachtas members. A decision, of sorts, had been made, with attention now being able to be placed on the remaining days of the Dáil, passing the Finance Bill and whatever Green bills it was possible to get over the line by then.

The party was not overburdened with expectation. The predominant feeling was that the worst was behind us, and that we could prepare for whatever fate held in store for us. Or so we thought.

We met as a parliamentary party on 5th January 2011, and election preparations continued. Confusion over the ambiguity of the 22nd November 2010 statement was still being dealt with. On the legislation front there seemed to be a few shafts of light.

The Local Government (Mayor and Regional Authority of Dublin) Bill had had a second stage debate in the Dáil in November. On 7th January, the Environment (Miscellaneous Provisions) Bill dealing with waste levies, especially an incinerator levy, was published. Debating time had been made available to move the Climate Change Bill in the Seanad on 13th January.

The bill that the Greens most wanted to see enacted was making slower progress. Heads of Bill had been prepared and agreed for a Corporate Donations Bill, but publishing the bill and processing it through both Houses of the Oireachtas was becoming less likely.

With the Finance Bill, the sole official reason for remaining in government, progress was not as smooth as it could have been either. A loophole had arisen where application of the Universal Social Charge would see those with incomes over €100,000 a year pay proportionately less. Behind closed doors we were insisting that this loophole could not remain. As with much of what we sought to change while in government, bringing those changes about internally meant that no credit for the change ever attached to the Green Party. It was the Greens continuing failure to highlight our own achievements that dogged us until the end of our period in government.

The more serious argument on the Finance Bill related to a proposal to delay the extinguishing of the controversial Section 23 property tax relief. Strong lobbying accompanied this new inclusion in the Finance Bill. For the Greens, it seemed to be yet another instance of catering to a lobbying group, whose activities had caused so much damage to the economy. Fianna Fáil wanted an open ended investigation into the effects of extinguishing this tax relief. The Greens wanted any investigation, which we felt to be spurious in any case, to be time limited. The ability to extinguish this relief in 2011 had to remain.

These issues would have been difficult enough, but manageable on their own. The weekend would see another soap opera twist that would contribute to making the final days in government unbearable.

The Sunday Times reported that Brian Cowen had played golf with key Anglo Irish director Sean Fitzpatrick in June 2008, weeks before the crucial decision to implement a bank guarantee was made. It wasn't known what was said or what had happened that day. What it did was feed a perception of the intricate relationship that continued to exist between key figures in Fianna Fáil and Anglo Irish Bank, as well as create an impression that failure to legally act against certain individuals was informed by these relationships.

Once again Brain Cowen was on the back foot, and once again the Greens were expected to act in a certain way. Our final parliamentary party think-in was taking place this week at the Grand Hotel in Malahide. Yet again, instead of being able to put forward the best case possible for the Green Party on what we were achieving and what we wanted to achieve, we were reacting to what was happening in Fianna Fáil and defending the Greens' continued participation in government.

I spent the morning of our think-in at the RTÉ radio studio in Donnybrook, along with Fianna Fáil's Noel Dempsey, taking part in a segment on the *Today with Pat Kenny* show on negotiating a programme for government. We skirted around the issue of Brian Cowen's golf playing partners. I expressed my own unhappiness, but equally stressed that it was an issue for Brian Cowen to sort out.

Pat Kenny, with an upcoming election in mind, wanted to probe the mechanics of a programme for government negotiation. Noel Dempsey said that the Greens, because of being more 'ideological', were the most difficult party with whom he had negotiated. I doubt if that was true. He went on to say that the Greens were also unrealistic in our expectation as to how policy can be progressed. Statements like this, verging on the patronising, seemed to typify Fianna Fáil's attitude towards the Greens.

When I got back to Malahide, the parliamentary party was once more between the proverbial rock and the hard place. This was a government that was now on a limited time-scale. In normal circumstances, the Greens would have left the government after revelations like those from *The Sunday Times*, but to leave now without completing the one thing we believed needed to be done – passing a Finance Bill – would subject the party to even more ridicule.

The press conference that followed the think-in, exemplified by John Gormley's exasperated remark 'last time it was Garglegate; this time it's Golfgate' was a thoroughly depressing affair. It wasn't even enlivened by a Sinn Féin stunt that preceded it.

Back in Leinster House on the following day, the meetings continued. Brian Cowen had made a statement on his meeting with Sean Fitzpatrick. The Green position was that Cowen's had to be a matter for Fianna Fáil. The Greens were being reassured by Fianna Fáil that the Finance Bill would be processed by March. As well the Green pieces of legislation, the party was also pushing for the Children's Rights referendum to coincide with a general election.

Rumblings continued on the following day. Fianna Fáil back-benchers began to make their discontent known. A Fianna Fáil parliamentary party meeting would be held that afternoon. The Green Party's belief was that at that meeting Cowen's leadership of Fianna Fáil would be over. In his interactions with him, John Gormley noted how broken a man Brian Cowen had become. He seemed utterly without support, even within his own party. He spoke openly with John, claiming by then that there was no one in his party with whom he was able to speak in that way.

At the Greens' parliamentary party meeting, the various options were discussed:

John Gormley: Cowen gone as Fianna Fáil leader... Are we okay to continue? What are we saying publicly?

Dan Boyle: Caretaker Taoiseach and definite date set for election. Express our discomfort at the situation.

Eamon Ryan: We have three choices: accept Cowen as caretaker Taoiseach; elect a new Taoiseach (which we can't do); or have a General Election.

Dan Boyle: We can't allow Cowen to stay on as caretaker Taoiseach when it's clear that his own party do not have confidence in him.

Niall O'Brolchain: Agree with Dan.

Paul Gogarty: In the national interest the Finance Bill has to be passed – this has been our mantra. We can't get involved in internal Fianna Fáil matters. Focus on the passage of the Finance Bill; it's crucial for the country's recovery.

Mary White: I agree with Paul, we have to maintain some level of consistency. We can't falter now. We have curtailed the lifetime of the government.

Niall O'Brolchain: Another option is to support the passage of the Finance Bill from outside of government.

Mary White: And then we lose all our legislation?

Eamon Ryan: Be careful about our legislation – the Finance Bill must be of primary concern. What would happen if the Finance Bill was not passed?

Dan Boyle: 1987 Fine Gael and Labour coalition sets a precedent for an interim government with a caretaker Taoiseach. We can point to this model.

Trevor Sargent: We cannot vote confidence in Cowen as Taoiseach. If he resigns as Taoiseach we can vote for a caretaker and get legislation through.

John Gormley: At this stage, all options outlined look impossible for us.

Dan Boyle: Only one scenario could possibly work at this stage: new Fianna Fáil leader, new caretaker Taoiseach

and a definite election date. We can say that we can no longer support Cowen as he twice withheld information.
John Gormley: What does Paul think?
Paul Gogarty: We need to keep our counsel for the moment. It's up to Fianna Fáil to appoint a caretaker Taoiseach. We need to remain consistent on the passage of the Finance Bill.
Donal Geoghegan: Two key points to bear in mind: have to maximise changes for success in general election and use our leverage to get key legislation through between now and then. We have more leverage now than we did a few hours ago, and need to use it to maximum effect.

We agreed that John Gormley and Mary White should meet with Micheál Martin (now seen as the most likely caretaker), with Tony Killeen to state that the Greens would support a caretaker Taoiseach as long as definitive election date would be set.

The outcome from the Fianna Fáil parliamentary party meeting was confused. Brian Cowen would be staying on for the moment. He would be consulting on a one-to-one basis in the coming days with members of the Fianna Fáil parliamentary party.

Colm O'Caomhanaigh: What is the least damaging option for us now?
John Gormley: Voting confidence in Cowen would be the most damaging. The members have had enough and won't support the parliamentary party if we vote confidence in him. There is a real credibility issue with either voting confidence or voting for a new Taoiseach.
Dan Boyle: I can't honestly see how we can support Cowen at this stage. We are close to breaking point. It's

a matter of pride. There has been an accumulation of issues.

John Gormley: The message for heading into the election must be that we can't support Cowen. That will resonate with people. We need to get out on the doorsteps now and consult locally.

Paul Gogarty: We have played the national interest card. If a decision is made to leave government, it has to happen before a Labour motion of no confidence.

Ciarán Cuffe: Can John go to Cowen and ask for election date to be set?

John Downing: That would be helpful, in particular in putting some structure on the situation in the media.

The second-stage debate on the Climate Change Bill began on this day in the Seanad. Emboldened by comments made by some interest groups, particularly the IFA, but the IBEC as well, some Fianna Fáil senators began sticking their heads above the parapet. The leadership vacuum in Fianna Fáil allowed them even more scope to do so. Most attention continued to be focussed on events within Fianna Fáil. On Saturday 15th, the Green parliamentary party held a teleconference.

John Gormley: Tony Killeen says Cowen is receiving a mixture of feedback regarding staying or going. Is it best for us if he stays?

Eamon Ryan: Go as leader of Fianna Fáil and stay as Taoiseach would be the best scenario for us.

John Gormley: Getting the election date confirmed remains of paramount importance.

Paul Gogarty: If it goes to a motion of confidence or no confidence, what is our position?

*Ciarán Cuffe: We can't make a decision until all informa-
tion is available, and we're not there yet.*
*John Gormley: An option is to table a countermotion
saying confidence in the government to continue until
March?*
*Dan Boyle: Yes, and secure a date at the same time. We
can't do anything further for the moment.*

On Sunday the 16th, Green Party Oireachtas members came
to Government Buildings to discuss ever-changing developments:

*John Gormley: This is the updated position. Cowen is to
stay on and reshuffle the Cabinet. Can we stay? It will
all come down to the confidence question.*
Colm O'Caomhanaigh: Why reshuffle now?
*John Gormley: Positions are being offered in return for
offers of support.*
Colm O'Caomhanaigh: Disastrous messaging.
*Mary White: Nothing has changed. If he is staying and
people resign, they have to be replaced. We should stick
to seeking the election date to be confirmed.*
*John Gormley: It keeps coming back to the same ques-
tion. What is best for us at this stage?*
*John Downing: The parliamentary party has managed
the situation well so far, but absolutely the date needs
to be confirmed as soon as possible. We need to say
something strong in the media today.*
*John Gormley: I will go back to Cowen and will say that
it is imperative we have an election date and a commitment to progress on legislation.*
*Donal Geoghegan: It is vital that the date does not
go into April, and cannot be vague either. Set for 25th*

*March. John should also suggest that a reshuffle would
not play well and that he should temporarily take on the
portfolio of any minister who resigns.*

John Gormley returned to the meeting at 5.30 having spoken
with Brian Cowen. He reported that Brian Cowen was to
put a motion of confidence to the Fianna Fáil parliamentary
party on Tuesday. As this was an unusual move, he must have
been confident of winning:

*Eamon Ryan: The less we say the better for the
moment.*
*John Gormley: I have spoken to Brian Lenihan. It is likely
that Fianna Fáil ministers who resign will be replaced for
the election, and that they will try and push the date out
into April. We have to harden our attitude now and use
our leverage to maximum effect. It's time to suggest that
the Finance Bill might not go through.*
*Eamon Ryan: We absolutely cannot go beyond March,
but must be careful on Finance Bill shift, we cannot
speak publicly to this.*
*Dan Boyle: We need to make a statement regarding the
election date this evening.*
*John Gormley: I would rather meet Cowen face to face
to confirm the date in the morning and make a statement then.*
*Paul Gogarty: To confirm the strategy… if we can't get a
clear answer re the date of the election we go?*
*John Downing: We'll put out a holding statement for the
media this evening 'Green Party TDs and Senators this
evening discussed the Taoiseach's statement. The Green
Party has stood back to allow Fianna Fáil to deal with*

its own affairs. We believe that there must be an early resolution to this situation.'

On Monday, positioning himself for the post-Cowen future in Fianna Fáil, Micheál Martin announced that he would not be supporting the motion of confidence. Despite this, on Tuesday the Fianna Fáil parliamentary party voted confidence in Cowen, probably deciding that it was now too late to change leader before the election. He was ebullient.

John Gormley was speaking to Brian Cowen after the vote, and learned that he intended to go ahead with a full-scale Cabinet reshuffle. The Greens continued to strongly oppose the idea. Donal Geoghegan was suggesting that the Taoiseach was being advised internally not to proceed with this idea. The Greens continued to hope that the Taoiseach would see sense.

A meeting was organised for early on Wednesday morning on the subject of timetabling the remaining legislation. It was held in the Taoiseach's office in Government Buildings. With the Taoiseach were the Government Chief Whip John Curran and the Minister for Defence Tony Killeen. The Green Party delegation comprised of John Gormley, Eamon Ryan and me.

My attendance was last minute as the Green Party Whip Trevor Sargent, who was meant to attend, found himself with a heavy head cold and asked me to attend in his stead as I had a good understanding of parliamentary procedure. The atmosphere was businesslike, if a little tense. Brian Cowen was in confident form. We expressed our fear that the Climate Change Bill was being attacked by Fianna Fáil senators despite it being an important part of the programme for government. We seemed to get an assurance that the message would be given to the Fianna Fáil parliamentary party to that effect.

With that item dealt with, Brian Cowen turned to the issue that was most important to him. We were informed that the ministerial resignation of Mícheál Martin would be added to with the impending resignations of Dermot Ahern and Noel Dempsey, both of whom had indicated that they wouldn't be contesting the next general election. Tony Killeen, at the meeting, indicated that he too would be resigning for the same reason. Brian Cowen wanted to replace all of the resigning ministers and possibly others, but for the moment at least he would take over the Foreign Affairs portfolio.

Each of the Greens present informed him that this wasn't a good idea – that we didn't support it; that it would create a 'jobs for the boys' perception with the general public, and that, more importantly, it would sow the seed that the life of the government was being unnecessarily prolonged. We repeated our belief that any vacant portfolios should be redistributed amongst the remaining members of the Cabinet for the remaining time available to the government.

I told the Taoiseach that a motion brought before the House on approving a new Cabinet would effectively be a vote of confidence in the government, and that was something our parliamentary party would have great difficulty in supporting.

We left that meeting convinced that the Taoiseach had heard our concerns and was reconsidering his plans. Brian Cowen was given space by the Greens. As I left the meeting, I had concerns that if this represented the regular dialogue between the parties I could see how problems had arisen. The style on the part of the Greens was far too deferential and not nearly challenging enough.

A Green parliamentary party meeting directly followed. Eamon Ryan reported that the Climate Change Bill would conclude in the Seanad on the following day, and that a meeting of the Fianna Fáil parliamentary party on that evening would be informed by the Taoiseach that the bill had to be proceeded with. The issue of whether the Taoiseach would or would not go ahead with a disastrous Cabinet reshuffle most exercised the collective mind of the Green parliamentary party.

John Gormley: This reshuffle issue is really growing legs. The election date has not been addressed clearly. We are still receiving strong advice to get out. What do we do?

Paul Gogarty: We should begin to plan for going to the country next Wednesday. We must request that the date be confirmed. If the Taoiseach refuses to confirm then say we can't vote confidence.

Eamon Ryan: We need to point out that it hasn't been too bad a day today! The Climate Change Bill is out of the Seanad; we've got our way on Section 23 and we're out there on getting the date confirmed. We need to remain cautious, though, as the Finance Bill has to be passed.

Paul Gogarty: If we don't have a date by the time of the motion [of confidence] next week then we have to go. We will have no leverage left at that stage. No credibility either.

John Gormley: Do we want to be in the government when the election is called? We can pass the Finance Bill from opposition benches…

Eamon Ryan: We're still making progress. We can get two out of three pieces of legislation through if we hold our nerve. That would be a much better narrative for election time than the current, chaotic narrative.

Brian Cowen had gone from the meeting with the Greens into the Dáil chamber, where he delivered a knockabout performance that left many thinking that he had regained his old swagger. But this was hubris; not confidence.

That evening, events seemed to move from the farcical to the surreal. John Gormley appeared on the *Six One News* on RTÉ Television. He tried to pour cold water on the idea of a major Cabinet reshuffle. A vacancy existed because of the resignation of Micheál Martin. A further vacancy could arise after the hospitalisation of Dermot Ahern, who was taking respite for a minor health condition. For revealing this information, John Gormley was later to receive a very irate phone call from Dermot Ahern, confirming that he was very capable of continuing with his ministerial responsibilities.

On the *Nine O'Clock News*, Mary Harney announced her resignation. She had seen John Gormley a number of hours previously, but had said nothing. Her resignation was added to those of Noel Dempsey, Tony Killeen and Dermot Ahern.

By morning, the resignation of Batt O'Keeffe had also been announced. It was clear by now that considerable choreography was afoot. It was also obvious that the Taoiseach had heard the Greens' concerns but had chosen to ignore them, believing that the party should remain in government under any circumstances in order to pass what it believed to be important legislation.

At 7a.m., John Gormley angrily phoned the Taoiseach and demanded to know what was going on. Paul Gogarty was on the *Morning Ireland* programme, emphatically stating that the Greens would not support a wide-scale Cabinet reshuffle.

On going into Leinster House, I met with Micheál Martin at the Kildare Street gate. A photographer from *The Irish Times* captured that meeting. My arms were outstretched. I was saying to him 'What the hell is going on, Micheál? What does he think he's doing?' From where Micheál Martin was sitting, these were probably metaphorical questions. Brian Cowen's behaviour was suiting him down to the ground.

The Green parliamentary party met very early that morning. The tension was acute.

> *John Gormley: The Taoiseach is to put the motion [on new ministerial appointments] on the Order Paper this morning. It is a very bad idea.*
> *Paul Gogarty: Put a two-week deadline for the Finance Bill to the Taoiseach today.*
> *Trevor Sargent: Patience is gone at this stage. The Climate Change Committee was humiliating yesterday [Trevor had been the only government representative defending the bill there]. Appointing new ministers is completely unnecessary. The Taoiseach can double up on positions.*
> *Niall O'Brolchain: At this stage we are not in government any more. We are now in an election campaign.*
> *Ciarán Cuffe: Paul was right to go out on radio this morning, and he was right in what he said. Now we need to proceed carefully. We absolutely cannot accept where we are at now.*
> *John Gormley: The only option now is to leave government and support the Finance Bill from the opposition. All agreed?*
> *Eamon Ryan: What about the other pieces of legislation?*

To this final question, all others present agreed that it was too late now. John rang the Taoiseach from the meeting to say that the Green Party would not accept new ministerial appointments. He told the party, 'He's not putting it on the Order Paper now. We need to get him to announce that he's not doing it.'

John went to meet directly with the Taoiseach. The party chose to stay out of the chamber for the order of business. He returned, saying 'The Taoiseach is still pushing ahead. He's saying that the new ministers won't get salaries etc. The letters of resignation have not gone to the President yet. There is a still an opportunity to stop this.'

The shuttle diplomacy continued with John Gormley going to the Taoiseach's office a number of other times, firstly with Mary White, and later these two were joined by Eamon Ryan. In the meantime, John received a phone call from Brian Lenihan stating that it was not possible for the ministers to stay on at this stage. After these contacts the Green parliamentary party resumed.

> *Eamon Ryan: We still want to see Finance Bill through.*
> *Trevor Sargent: We don't have to be in government to do this. Fianna Fáil is in freefall. The new appointments will accentuate fractures. We cannot remain part of this coalition.*

It was agreed to reach out to Fine Gael and Labour to arrange the passage of the Finance Bill.

> *John Gormley: When do we make the announcement? We are taking the decision to leave government today? Agreed?*

It was. The Green Party's press officer Damian Connon was asked to draft a short press release stating that the

Government was no longer workable; that it was beyond repair. The party would call on the opposition to support the passage of Finance Bill. A press conference was to be organised for the Leinster House plinth later that day. Gormley was to go to the Taoiseach and inform him of our decisions. When he returned, there was yet another twist in the tale.

John Gormley: The Taoiseach won't make the new appointments. What now?
Dan Boyle: It's still time to go.
Eamon Ryan: Don't do anything immediately. Wait an hour or two. Talk to Kenny and Gilmore.
John Gormley: It's time for level heads for now. No communications for the moment.

The monitor in John Gormley's office, which had been muted, had its sound restored on noticing Brian Cowen re-entering the Dáil chamber.

The Taoiseach: I wish to announce for the information of the House that the President, acting on my advice, has accepted the resignations of Deputies Mary Harney, Noel Dempsey, Dermot Ahern, Batt O'Keeffe and Tony Killeen as members of the Government. I advised the House yesterday of the resignation of Deputy Micheál Martin. I want to put on the record of the House my gratitude to each of them for their distinguished contributions to the work of the Government and the country.

The Minister for Health and Children, Deputy Mary Harney, has advanced a strategic approach to tackling the problems in our health services. She has done a first class job and shown extraordinary endurance and intelligence in dealing with our most challenging portfolio.

In her previous work as Minister for Enterprise, Trade and Employment and Tánaiste she made an enduring contribution to developing the economic base of the country.

Deputy Noel Dempsey has served this country well in a variety of portfolios. At the Cabinet table he was a straight talking and respected colleague, forceful in his contributions and a loyal supporter of Government decisions. His achievements as a Minister are many. As Minister for Transport he brought forward significant legislation and initiatives which have reduced the number of road deaths in Ireland, thus saving many lives.

Deputy Dermot Ahern has been a reforming Minister for Justice and Law Reform who carried out his duties with great ability and commitment to the public good. He, too, has many achievements, including the recent groundbreaking anti-gangland legislation. I also served with Dermot in the Governments of Deputy Bertie Ahern and saw at first hand the strong contribution he made to the Irish peace process from its inception in his role as envoy for the UN Secretary General.

As Minister for Foreign Affairs, Deputy Micheál Martin has represented the country with distinction at home and abroad. I especially want to place on the record of the House my gratitude to him for the work he has done to bring further significant progress in the political landscape in Northern Ireland. The Hillsborough agreement last February opened a new and positive chapter for the people of Northern Ireland, and Micheál's political skills were crucial to that outcome. Deputy Martin is a politician of substance who has served the people extremely well in the Departments of Education and

Science, Enterprise, Trade and Employment, Health and Children and Foreign Affairs.

Deputy Batt O'Keeffe has been one of my best friends in politics and in life. He is a politician of great wisdom, intelligence and loyalty. He has been a hard-working public representative for over a quarter of a century and he has come to a decision not to contest the next election. From our discussions I know he shares my assessment that there is a need to have more young people in Government as a necessary source of renewal and vitality in our politics. He has made a major contribution to the Government. As Minister for Education and Science he placed at centre stage the debate on how we are to resource our universities and institutes of technology to make them the best in the world. He embarked on radical programmes of school curriculum reform, including project maths. As Minister for Enterprise, Trade and Innovation he ensured significant and tailored investment in the enterprise and innovation agencies which are now helping to drive export-led recovery. He turned a policy focus on commercialised research and set in motion the implementation of the report of the innovation task force.

It was my great pleasure to appoint Deputy Tony Killeen as the Minister for Defence in March last year. Although his time in the Department of Defence was brief, he was responsible for a number of significant developments. He oversaw the successful completion of the Defence Forces UN mission from Chad last summer and announced a new peacekeeping deployment to the Lebanon before Christmas. Overall, his was a wise and sensible voice at Cabinet during some of the most challenging times ever faced by an Irish Government.

I want again to express my attitude to each of the aforementioned Deputies and wish them well for the future. We in this House are all aware of the immense challenges each and every member of this Administration has faced in charting a way through some of the most difficult economic times since the foundation of the State. History will show that the Government has worked hard in the national interest to implement difficult but necessary decisions to help lead our country through an international economic and financial crisis, the likes of which we have not seen in over eighty years. The Government, under my leadership, has followed a consistent path to help stabilise the economy in the aftermath of the biggest downturn in modern Irish economic history.

Our budgetary strategy has helped to stabilise the economy and return it to economic growth. I understand that people are suffering and experiencing immense hardship because of the recession, which we deeply regret. It is incumbent on all of us in public office to put the interests of the country above everything else. Politics as usual should not be allowed to distract from the overriding priority of getting Ireland back on track. As I said previously, there will be a general election this spring but before that the Government has important work to complete.

The Government has obtained approval for its national recovery plan, providing for the proper funding of the State through the negotiation of the EU and IMF package. It will give us time and space to continue on the path of adjustment to restore economic growth and thereby create jobs. It will allow us to continue to bring our public finances back to order while providing necessary public services for our people. It is important in the weeks ahead that the Government gives legislative effect to the budget through the enactment of the finance Bill and other related Bills which benefit the people. There is nothing more important than doing precisely that.

In the interest of proper governance, I have decided to reassign the portfolios of those Ministers who have resigned. Pursuant to section 4(1) of the Ministers and Secretaries (Amendment) Act 1946, I am assigning their Departments as follows: the Department of Health and Children to the Tánaiste and Minister for Education and Skills, Deputy Mary Coughlan; the Department of Transport to the Minister for Community, Equality and Gaeltacht Affairs, Deputy Pat Carey; the Department of Justice and Law Reform to the Minister for Agriculture, Fisheries and Food, Deputy Brendan Smith; the Department of Enterprise, Trade and Innovation to the Minister for Tourism, Sport and Culture, Deputy Mary Hanafin; and the Department of Defence to the Minister for Social Protection, Deputy Éamon Ó Cuív.

From the outset, the main task of the Government I have led has been to secure the best interests of the nation in these challenging times. We have made hard choices and taken unpopular decisions, in the interest of the security and well-being of the people. I believe the best interests of Ireland demand that Government gets on with implementing the national recovery plan, by passing the Finance Bill and other legislation and that a new Government then receives a new mandate from the people at a general election. Until then, as Taoiseach, my priorities, along with those of my Government colleagues, will continue to be returning Ireland to recovery, *creating jobs and restoring the public finances. It is my intention in due course to seek a dissolution of Dáil Éireann, with a view to a general election taking place on Friday, 11 March next. Prior to the general election, we are committed to enacting key pieces of legislation to secure Ireland's economic future.*

I know that the Government's policies are returning Ireland to recovery and growth and I want us to get through the hard times and see the country prosper in the future. To do that, we need now at this crucial time to get on with the important work in hand. As Taoiseach, my focus today and every day until election day is on completing the work I have undertaken on behalf of the people to continue the process of implementing the economic recovery plan.

In John Gormley's office we sat in stunned disbelief. The reshuffle had not happened. We finally had a date for a general election. Ministerial portfolios had been reallocated, pointedly not to either Green Party minister, not that that mattered. There was also a feeling that additional pieces of legislation were unlikely to be passed now.

> *Eamon Ryan: Now we have what we wanted: a date set, no new appointments, no motion.*
> *Paul Gogarty: Now we don't get the credit for ending.*
> *John Gormley: Is this a win? Enough of a win to stay in government?*

It was felt that it was; at least for now.

> *Trevor Sargent: But I feel a trap is being set by Fianna Fáil to force us to go on the Climate Change Bill instead.*

Discussion continued on holding a more detailed press conference that afternoon. The venue now was to be the Merrion Hotel. In that room, the remaining acts of the life of this government would be played out. At 4.30p.m., the Green parliamentary party met a packed collection of reporters. I sat, as Chair of the party, in the centre of a front table, John Gormley to my right, Mary White to his right and Eamon Ryan to my left.

The mood from the media had been less hostile than we had experienced in the previous months. There was some sense as to what we were still doing in government. The questions were polite, asking what it was we knew, what it was we said and when. For the most part, there seemed to be an acceptance that we hadn't been treated fairly.

That evening I had a less benign experience on the *Tonight with Vincent Browne* programme on TV3. Vincent openly challenged my account of the meeting that had taken place on Wednesday morning.

'Who was at the meeting, Vincent, me or you?' I challenged him. On the same programme was Fianna Fáil's Conor Lenihan, who later took the opportunity of challenging Vincent even more aggressively. Vincent is a very effective journalist and is very entertaining, but at that stage I had taken all I was prepared to take.

On Friday we met again as a parliamentary party, realising that all had changed, but still trying to affect a business-as-usual approach. Once again we waited while Fianna Fáil decided what it was to do.

John Downing: We're doing well so far.
Mark Dearey: I had a difficult local radio interview yesterday on us not walking out of government.

Ciarán Cuffe: The Finance Bill and its passage remains the only defence.

Trevor Sargent: The importance of the Finance Bill is clear to all. My local group say that we can't waver on seeing the Finance Bill through at this stage.

John Gormley: If we go without getting the Finance Bill through...?

Donal Geoghegan: We will be charged with inconsistency.

What these accounts of the last three months of Green parliamentary party meetings may not fully get across is the sense of pressure that each of us felt, staff as well as parliamentarians. There was Mary White telling of being spat at by a constituent; Mark Dearey talking about meeting a supporter and plaintively asking his Green colleagues 'How can I be able to look him in the eye?'

While meeting piled upon meeting gave a sense of things being *ad hoc*, Donal Geoghegan and Aoife Ní Lochlainn strove hard to keep a logic to the proceedings. Donal produced reams and reams of review documents. The press officers John Downing, Liam Reid, Bríd McGrath, Damian Connon and Nicola Cassidy had to react to often hourly changing events. The Green Leinster House and constituency office staff dealt with an angry public that was growing angrier by the day with a grace which still left them all diminished. For that, we were subject to a mixture of ridicule and indifference, with scarcely an acknowledgement that we were doing the best we could under the worst set of circumstances.

We all felt our bruises. Brian Cowen must have felt even worse. Having renewed his mandate as Fianna Fáil leader, for reasons only known to himself he threw that all away in an instant and restored all the previous doubts.

On Saturday he came to the Merrion Hotel to make his statement that he was resigning as Fianna Fáil leader. Green Oireachtas members listened to his statements in different parts of the country. Each of us knew that one final act had to follow. We gathered again for one last time at Government Buildings on Sunday.

A Taoiseach no longer leader of his party meant a government of which we could no longer be a part. We met to discuss the how, no longer the when, and long since had passed the time of seeking the why. Could the Finance Bill still be passed? Eamon Ryan had initiated contact with Fine Gael's Simon Coveney. It seemed likely that co-operation on that would be forthcoming.

Drafting the letters of resignation from John, Eamon, Mary and Ciaran took longer than had been thought. While we waited, all of us walked around aimlessly in the corridor outside the offices where Green Party staff worked. We made occasional half-hearted pieces of conversation of not much consequence, then waited and waited for our collective date with destiny.

We walked together from the door of Government Buildings through the courtyard, then across Merrion Street to the Merrion Hotel, our every step being recorded by cameras. The room where the previous press conferences had been was packed once again with journalists. This time instead of a top table there was a small podium.

We gathered around that podium. I introduced John, after which he read out his prepared statement. Questioning afterwards was brief and very polite. This one, rare occasion managed to become imbued with a dignity that we had found so lacking for so long. This was John Gormley's statement:

On November 22 last we said that an election should be held early this year because of the events surrounding the IMF bailout. On that occasion we identified four key priorities, which needed to be addressed before this election could take place. These were: concluding financial arrangements with the EU/IMF; producing a four year economic plan; passing Budget 2011; and passing the Finance Bill to give effect to that Budget.

Today, three of these four objectives have been completed. We believe it is possible to complete the Finance Bill quickly before going to a general election.

We believe that this election is absolutely necessary. The Irish people have begun to lose confidence in politics and in the political process. They have watched aghast the conduct in Dáil Éireann of political parties.

The Irish people expect and deserve better.

For a very long time we in the Green Party have stood back in the hope that Fianna Fáil could resolve persistent doubts about their party leadership. A definitive resolution of this has not yet been possible, and our patience has reached an end.

Because of these continuing doubts, the lack of communication and the breakdown in trust, we have decided that we can no longer continue in government.

We will remain true to our promise to support the Finance Bill from the opposition benches, with the promised co-operation of the opposition parties. Yesterday, Eamon Ryan initiated contact with the main opposition party in this regard, and they have undertaken to facilitate the passage of the Finance Bill.

I understand that similar undertakings have now been given by other opposition parties.

We hope that they will keep their word.

We also hope that the Fianna Fáil party will make every effort to fast-track this legislation.

It has been a very rare privilege to serve in government. It would of course have been preferable if our time in government had not coincided with the worst economic downturn in our nation's history. It has meant having to take the most difficult decisions that any party could have faced.

We did so it was because it was the right thing to do.

I am proud of our many achievements in the areas of planning, renewable energy, energy standards of buildings, water conservation and other environmental areas. I'm proud that we gave rights to gay couples through civil partnership, and that we persisted in our belief that education and the arts should be protected. These two areas are absolutely vital for our economic recovery.

I regret, obviously, that we did not have more time to complete our other legislation, which is very well advanced.

I would like to thank our party members for their steadfast and loyal support in the face of unprecedented challenges. I'd like to thank our hard-working staff and our families who have had to endure the pressures that go with being in government.

Our record is one of responsibility, reform, steadfastness and creativity.

And these are the very characteristics that will enable this country to get back on a path of sustainable recovery, underpinned by a very different set of values.

Go raibh mile maith agaibh.

***

The deed done, for the Green Oireachtas members the remaining week of the 30th Dáil was something of a blur. I wrote my letter of resignation as Deputy Leader of Seanad Éireann two days after the party left government. I hadn't really given it any thought. I did, though, receive a very kind letter from Brian Cowen in return.

Fianna Fáil turned to Micheál Martin as its saviour. The opposition negotiated an election two weeks earlier as their price for facilitating the passage of Finance Bill. Two days in the Dáil was followed by a final day's debate in the Seanad.

Brian Lenihan was assured as the last chapter of the Finance Bill was played out in the Seanad. I was disappointed that he chose to make a negative reference to the Green Party not allowing more time for all details of the Finance Bill to be included. These related to many of the tax provisions resulting from the Civil Partnership Act. Not being able to give immediate effect to that Bill disappointed us too, but the timetabling of the Finance Bill was more a matter of what had been agreed with the opposition parties. In my contribution on the Finance Bill I tried to get these points across. This was the bill, and these were the issues that overshadow and most probably prolonged our time in government:

Senator Dan Boyle: The Finance Bill 2011 and the circumstances arising from it consist of two very separate issues. The first is the need to pass the Bill to give a sense of certainty, cohesion and continuity to the very uncertain political and economic situation in which the country finds itself. The second relates to the contents of the Bill, and it is here there can be legitimate public debate about the nature of the economy and how the burden is being shared between all citizens.

We can describe the Finance Bill 2011 as probably the longest death-wish in Irish political history. Unlike previous Finance Acts that were passed before the 2002 and 2007 elections, this is hardly an election Bill. When I think of those particular Acts and the budgets that accompanied them in 2001 and 2006, we can see how radically the situation has changed. Public expenditure increased by 20% in 2002 alone, which was far in excess of the rate of inflation. In 2006, public expenditure increased by 14%, which again was far in excess of the rate of inflation. These exercises were nothing less than the traditional attempt to buy the subsequent election. While we might concentrate on the banking mess that occurred since, the reality is that our biggest problem is our public finances and this has been caused by a decade or more of spending too much and taxing too little.

Until we address that essential truth, much of the name-calling and points-scoring will be fundamentally dishonest in this debate.

I put it to Members that where we will be ending up in taxation and expenditure terms is probably where we should be. Pain is being caused because the adjustment is happening too quickly and is too much for many citizens. That is where the political debate needs to be. If we had not reduced taxes recklessly and if we had not increased expenditure in a naked attempt to buy political power, position and prestige, then we would not be in this position. We then have the banking mess on top of it.

Having said all that, it does not give my party any particular pleasure in agreeing to pass this Bill. However, it needs to be passed. The best achievement has been to get rid of some of the unwelcome signals that were coming out of the original draft of the Bill. These signals included the signal that those earning over €100,000 should not be charged an extra 3% in the universal social charge because it would affect the effective tax rate, the signal that there should not be a particular punitive rate of tax on bankers' bonuses, and the signal that the property tax reliefs in sections 22 and 23 could somehow be postponed into 2012. Those were unacceptable signals on top of a narrative where many of the citizens of this country were told that they had to bear a burden that others in our society were not expected to bear.

In leaving the Government, I am pleased that the Green Party challenged these particular provisions and we achieved amendments on them. There are others in the Lower House who have claimed this. Their involvement in those amendments was nil. I remember being involved in the negotiations on the formation of the Government and we expressed our concerns about the treatment of Independents supporting the previous Government. We did not want to be associated with that naked type of opportunism which accompanied the decisions of that Government. The strategy, as revealed at the time by Fianna Fáil, was that Independents did not effectively change anything but that decisions had already been made and the Independents were then given the opportunity to mouth off and say that they achieved those changes. The changes to property tax reliefs, to the taxation of bankers' bonuses and to impose a 3% charge for incomes in excess of €100,000 were effected by the Green Party. I particularly resent the views of Members of the Lower House who are *not known for their own adherence to the ideas of tax equity or even tax compliance claiming to be champions of the people in this area. On those grounds, we need to put aside the circus-like atmosphere that has attached to the Bill.*

There are some welcome elements in the Bill, most notably the excising and extinguishing of tax reliefs. The formation of the Commission on Taxation was a Green Party demand in the programme for Government. Its insistence that its recommendations be adhered to was something the Green Party in government called for, not only in this budget but in preceding budgets. It is again disappointing that it has taken the worsening of the crisis to implement many of these recommendations because they should have been implemented in 2008 and 2009. At least we are finally seeing light at the end of the tunnel. There is reason to take particular pleasure in seeing amendments to property-based tax reliefs in sections 22 and 23 which bring these reliefs to an end. There has been much lobbying on how individuals will be affected by these changes. Undoubtedly, some small-scale investors will feel the brunt of this particular change. However, the Green Party believes that this type of property tax relief was akin not so much to throwing petrol on a fire; more to setting fire to a refinery in terms of the effect it had in creating a property boom. We have had to live with the results of that since. The idea of a roll-over relief for properties already owned being added to new properties that were being created in a market for which there was no demand seems to epitomise everything that was wrong with the property-fuelled element of the Celtic tiger. That is why we should take some degree of pleasure from extinguishing those reliefs.

The other element of this Bill relates to the universal social charge and its effect. Undoubtedly, people on lower incomes are feeling this pinch more than others. However, there are good things to be said about it. The rationalisation of our levy system, whereby we have had an income levy, a health levy and PRSI as well as an insurance levy in the past, means that we need to get to a simplified system of one social insurance charge and one system of taxation. I would like to have seen that done in this budget. We have a half-a-horse approach on this and many other items in the Bill. We now have a USC, we now have PRSI and we now have income tax. It does not help the public mood, and if we were to have chosen reform, we should have done it in one bold leap.

One of the disappointments I have had as a party spokesperson in trying to influence budgets is the reluctance to embrace refundable tax credits, especially for the working poor. I would not lay the blame for this at the hands of the Minister, because I believe he is supportive of the idea. We proposed that this be introduced in the Bill at a cost of €100 per person, or a total cost of €60 million, increasing by the same amount over four years. In this way, a real benefit would be given to those at lower income levels. I am afraid that the people who opposed this the most are people in the Department of Finance.

I am disappointed with one thing the Minister said in respect of the Civil Partnership and Certain Rights and Obligations of Cohabitants Act 2010. He intimated that if the Green Party had given this Government another two to three weeks of artificial life, the measures in respect of that Act would have been brought into the Bill. I understand that at the meeting of all *party spokespersons a few days ago, it was commonly accepted that the 150 amendments relating to the Act can be introduced in the finance (No. 2) Bill, which can be passed before the first of April. I would like to see every political party commit to that. I welcome the fact that the Minister said he was surprised at the Green Party being seen in this position as the Green Party had pushed most strongly for the civil partnership legislation. This is something I did not hear from the relevant Minister at the time when he was finishing the debate on the Civil Partnership and Certain Rights and Obligations of Cohabitants Act 2010. On where we are as a country, in terms of the social aspects and taking responsibility for the financial difficulties we are in, my party has made sure that what can be done is being done. Those who will follow in the incoming Government will at least have a better base from which to improve on the policy mistakes made before we entered government.*

At the committee stage of the bill, the mood between Brian Lenihan and me deteriorated seriously. It was unfortunate and most likely unnecessary. Each of us, from our own party's perspective, wanted to make the government work. He could distance himself from the policies that had caused so much damage. In the end, the cultural differences between our parties was the largest reason why the government didn't work and couldn't work.

***

An unspoken irony of the Greens leaving government at that stage was that it would have been in Fianna Fáil's interest had the Greens left earlier. An earlier election would have seen more Fianna Fáil seats being won and with that a stronger platform from which to regroup.

Re-election for most of the Green TDs would have been difficult at any stage of the political cycle. A low voting base, combined with the loss of transfers and the disappearance of key sections of our voters, meant that the general election, when it came, would be virtually impossible for the party. All hopes rested with Eamon Ryan and Trevor Sargent being able to retain their seats in their Dublin constituencies.

In better circumstances, Mark Dearey would have strongly challenged for a Dáil seat in Louth. Fianna Fáil's Seamus Kirk becoming Ceann Comhairle, gaining automatic election, made things difficult enough, but the late introduction of Gerry Adams as the Sinn Féin candidate in the constituency made the uphill gradient for Mark even more severe.

That was the situation that faced the Green Party as a whole in the election. The added attention through daily live televised press conferences saw the party rise to 4% in the opinion polls, a figure that would have given the party a chance. Once the election was called that figure slipped and remained at 2%.

There was very little the party did wrong during the election campaign itself. Posters and election literature were well designed by our in-house designer Yvonne Loughrey. John Gormley had a very good election, performing very well in the Leaders' debate.

However, none of it mattered. Voters had already long decided what role the Green Party would play in the election. Canvassing in Cork South Central it became all too clear to me. There were few instances of real anger at the doorsteps. Indifference was more prevalent. Where refusals were given they were usually apologetic – We can't vote for you, Dan, not this time.

Election count day was made worse, not from the failed expectation of not winning a seat, but more from the scale of the drift of Green votes that occurred. In Cork South Central I lost two thirds of the votes I had won in 2007, and half of the votes I had won there as a candidate in the European election in 2009. It was a similar story for Green Party candidates throughout the country.

It became obvious early on during the counts that neither Eamon nor Trevor was going to make it. Green attention turned to maintaining a 2% vote share at which the party could continue to receive State funding. With two constituencies left to complete their first counts, the party slipped below that level. In the end, we were four thousand votes short of where we needed to be. Our humiliation was complete. Our road back would have to be from back where we started.

Two months remained in the life of the Seanad. As Party Chair, I thought it important that the party contest. There was little likelihood of success, but the logic was that if the Greens were to continue as a political party, elections should continue to be contested.

The hope was that Trevor Sargent would contest the Trinity College panel and Mark Dearey would be a candidate for the Industrial and Commercial panel. Trevor couldn't be persuaded. Mark was inclined but decided against. As the deadline for nominations was about to close, Niall O'Brolchain chose to contest the NUI panel while I contested the vocational panels.

From there it would be about reflection. John Gormley set the tone by not repeating the mistake Michael McDowell had made with the Progressive Democrats after the 2007 general election. There was no fit of pique; no histrionics. The transition was orderly.

A group of key party activists started an initiative, 'Regather and Refocus' bringing members together. It helped as it kept members together concentrating on what the party was and where it should be going.

Within three months, three hundred members met at the Hilton Hotel in Dublin to select a new leader. Eamon Ryan was elected, winning an election that included Kilkenny councillor Malcolm Noonan and longstanding activist Phil Kearney. My reason for not contesting was that after the general election I lacked the credibility to be the person to help the party restore its confidence. I looked for other ways in which I could contribute.

There was another contest for Deputy Leader, in which Catherine Martin was successful. In December, my term as Chair came to an end. I was replaced by Roderic O'Gorman. Catherine and Roderic represent a new generation in the Green Party, a generation committed to a political future for the party. Eamon Ryan later appointed party spokespersons who similarly were dedicated to that goal. Twelve months into its new life, not a lot had changed. The policies that existed while the Green Party were in government continued to be put in practice. The opposition parties that had tormented us while we were in government were behaving no differently. Knowing this is emboldening Green Party members who want to return to the fray do so having no confidence that other parties understand, or are in any way willing to implement, a Green agenda.

Postscript

In 2007 the party had the choice of whether it should become part of the government. The expectation was that it would be part of a Rainbow coalition. The choice that was available was with Fianna Fáil, the party that, to many Greens, represented much of what was wrong with Irish politics. After twenty-five years on the fringes of political life, the opportunity of government was one that the overwhelming number of party members felt should be taken.

The decision to enter government was made knowing that the party's vote and ability to win seats would be affected in the subsequent election. Part of that would be the swing that naturally occurs against incumbent government. The secondary factor was how the junior partner in coalition governments suffers disproportionately in Irish electoral contests. The most damaging factor for the Greens, though, was ceasing to be a transfer-friendly party, capable of picking up transfers from across the political spectrum. That ability had been crucial in winning the final seats in constituencies.

While the Greens had been critical of the direction of economic policy before entering government, few had realised how quickly and deeply the policy errors of previous governments had hurt the country. An irony was that the problems that began to surround the Irish economy, and then the economies of Greece, Portugal, Italy and Spain, were problems that all resulted from the weaknesses inherent in the foundation of the Euro as a currency. In the 1993 Irish referendum on the Treaty of Maastricht, the Green Party was the only party to effectively argue about the dangers that existed with the suggested approach towards creating a single currency.

The party allowed an impression to persist that economics was not part of its wider political agenda. That didn't stop the blame being apportioned when the economy came undone while the party was in government. Neither was any credit forthcoming for attempting to deal with the multiple economic crises.

The parallel narrative, fuelled by political opponents, was that the Greens were even failing on green issues. Rossport, Tara and Shannon became the mantra of those who wanted to portray the Greens in the worst possible light. No mercy was given on the issues of how little change had been achieved in each of these areas, notwithstanding how these issues were magnified to an importance they never really held within the Green Party's policy priorities.

Most of the period of government centred on economic crisis management, though, despite that, Green ministers fought hard to bring about changes in planning legislation, changing building regulations on energy efficiency and apartment size; in increasing renewable energy and insulating thousands of homes; and through introducing a significant piece of social legislation in the form of the Civil Partnership Bill. There was greater investment in water infrastructure; significant improvement in broadband speeds and access; a major review of broadcasting legislation. The house insulation programme created 6,000 unique jobs. The Bike to Work tax relief was shown to bring another 40,000 bikes back onto the roads. These are achievements in which, in the life of any other government, a great deal of pride could be taken.

When pressure was put to gain quick money through a fire sale of State assets, Eamon Ryan as the Minister responsible for many of those assets said these were vital and should remain in State ownership.

Important as many of those changes have been, the party in the general election of 2011 found itself on the wrong side of history. Now the party is reduced in the Republic to no more than a dozen local councillors, only three of whom are county councillors. Even at its lowest ebb, though, the party has found significant shafts of light.

As an all-Ireland party, real progress has been made in Northern Ireland. Away from the pressure of being associated with government, the Green Party has succeeded in winning a seat in the Northern Ireland Assembly twice. Brian Wilson in 2007, followed by Stephen Agnew in 2011 in the North Down constituency, were creating a niche in the still difficult sectarian environment of Northern Ireland politics. The election of a number of district councillors is solidifying a deepening presence there.

The first electoral test in the Republic since the general election of 2011 was the Dublin West by-election. For the first time in thirty years, the by-election was won by a candidate from a government party. Analysts expressed surprise at the strong performance of the Fianna Fáil candidate. In sixth position, ahead of the independent candidates, was the Green Party candidate Roderic O'Gorman. With 5% of the poll, Roderic was never challenging for the seat, but, in the aftermath of the Green Party's worst ever general election result, he had succeeded in delivering the best ever Green Party vote for that constituency – a harbinger for the future.

There are many reasons to believe that the Green Party will not go the way of previous minor parties in Irish politics. In the first instance, Greens are part of an international political movement that offers support and learning experiences. Green politics continues to grow as a political force in European politics. Despite this, many European Greens have also gone through the experience of gaining and then losing a parliamentary presence. In Germany, France, Italy, Sweden, the Czech Republic, Estonia and Belgium, Green parties gained a toehold only to find themselves subsequently out again in the political cold. Many of these parties came back again to gain greater political strength.

Secondly, the narrative in Irish politics will change. To what extent and by when is still unknown. At some stage, the blame attached to the last government will attach to some degree to the new government. Other political parties, still untainted by government, are better positioned to benefit from an ongoing anti-politics mood, but that pendulum will also begin to swing back. Some of what are now considered to be strong reasons against supporting the Greens will be reconsidered in a different light through the prism of time.

The third factor is an unwillingness of members to fold up tents. Membership remains solid, and people with enthusiasm to carry things forward abound within the party. Particularly encouraging is a younger generation of members who want to work to bring a more successful political future into being.

A fourth factor is a growing desire to go backwards to go forwards in the party; to reacquaint itself with its activist roots. In an age of uncertainty, where many citizens have turned away from conventional politics, partly through indifference and partly through distrust, the Green Party, once synonymous with being in the vanguard of non-conventional politics, needs to regain its cache.

If the party were to be sucked into the vortex that has swallowed several dozen minor parties before it, it could at least indulge itself in having taken the opportunity of entering government; of providing two well-performing Cabinet Ministers. In local government the party provided the Lord Mayor of Dublin and the Mayor of Galway, as well the first citizen in several other major urban centres like Dundalk, Bray and Kilkenny. The main reason the Greens will not suffer the same fate as other parties before it is that there is an unwillingness on the side of party members to indulge in the past.

When I'd lost my Dáil seat in 2007, I quoted from a Talking Heads song 'Once In A Lifetime'. Five years earlier during my acceptance speech on being elected to the Dáil, I quoted from one of my favourite Smiths songs, 'I was looking for a job, and then I found a job, and heaven knows I'm miserable now.' Now it seems more apt.

As we celebrate our 30th anniversary, neither the Greens nor the country are where we want them to be. From here we, as a party, will regroup and reorganise, believing in time that the sincerity we showed in government will contrast favourably with those other parties who, at the last election, chose to campaign on policies they knew could not be implemented. The environmental problems of the world have continued, and in many ways have worsened. While we live in a time of huge economic uncertainties, the need for a Green Party has never been greater. This is why we will continue to offer voters that alternative: because the need for that alternative has never been greater.

Was the party wrong to go into government in 2007? Did it linger there too long? The party could choose to dwell on these questions repetitively, or could choose to look instead to a future that remains uncertain but still requires a Green voice and a Green approach. Future participation in government is in a long distant future. Re-establishing a foothold in parliamentary life will prove difficult. What is certain is that the Green Party in Ireland will continue; that it is necessary; and that in future elections it will offer a choice.

The journey continues.

Index of Names